The Price of Mind: How Inflation Shapes Our Mental Worlds

Azhar ul Haque Sario

Copyright

Copyright © 2024 by Azhar ul Haque Sario

All rights reserved. No part of this book may be reproduced in any manner whatsoever without written permission except in the case of brief quotations embodied in critical articles and reviews.
First Printing, 2024

Azhar.sario@hotmail.co.uk

ORCID: https://orcid.org/0009-0004-8629-830X

Disclaimer: This book is free from AI use. The cover was designed in Microsoft Publisher.

Contents

Copyright 2
Chapter 1: The Burden of the Young 4
Chapter 2: Unequal Burdens 14
Chapter 3: The Gig Economy 23
Chapter 4: The Anxious Mind 31
Chapter 5: Panic Buying 39
Chapter 6: The Scarcity Trap 46
Chapter 7: Resilience in the Storm 55
Chapter 8: Community as Antidote 65
Chapter 9: Digital Lifeline 73
Chapter 10: Inflation and Social Unrest 83
Chapter 11: Trust in Crisis 91
Chapter 12: Political Polarization 99
Chapter 13: Rethinking Economic Policy 105
Chapter 14: Mental Healthcare in an Inflationary World 114
Chapter 15: The Double Bind 122
Chapter 16: The Metaverse 130
Chapter 17: Artificial Intelligence 139
About Author 147

Chapter 1: The Burden of the Young

The Thief of Time: How Inflation Steals Our Dreams

Inflation, that silent pickpocket, is robbing us of more than just our spending power. It's stealing our dreams, delaying our milestones, and forcing us to rewrite the timeline of our lives. Imagine it as a mischievous gremlin, gleefully inflating the cost of everything we hold dear, from the roof over our heads to the pitter-patter of tiny feet.

1. The Elusive Home: A Castle in the Clouds?

Remember playing house as a child, dreaming of the day you'd have your own place? Inflation has turned that dream into a moving target, a castle in the clouds that seems to float further away with each passing year.

The Price Tag Keeps Rising: It's like trying to catch a runaway train. Just as you save enough for a down payment, the house prices surge ahead, leaving you breathless and disheartened.
Mortgage Rates Bite: Adding insult to injury, interest rates soar, making those monthly payments a monstrous burden. Suddenly, that cozy cottage feels like a financial prison.
Leaky Roofs and Broken Dreams: Even if you manage to snag a home, the gremlin continues its torment. The cost of repairs and renovations skyrockets, turning every leaky faucet into a financial crisis.

Real-Life Woes:

In the US, the average age of first-time homebuyers is now a record high. Young adults are trapped in a cycle of rent, unable to save enough to escape.
The UK housing market is a battlefield, with fierce competition for affordable properties. "Generation Rent" is a grim reality, with many forced to postpone homeownership indefinitely.

2. Wedding Bells on Hold: Love in the Time of Inflation

Inflation isn't just a party pooper; it's a romance killer. Financial stress casts a long shadow over relationships, making it harder to say "I do."

Love vs. Money: The cost of living is a formidable opponent, forcing couples to choose between a dream wedding and a secure future. Romance often takes a backseat to practicality.
Career First, Family Later: In an uncertain economy, building a stable career becomes a priority. Marriage and family are postponed as individuals strive for financial independence.
Shifting Sands of Tradition: While marriage remains a cherished goal for many, societal norms are evolving. Cohabitation and other forms of commitment are gaining acceptance as inflation reshapes our choices.

The Data Speaks:

Marriage rates are declining globally, with financial concerns cited as a major culprit.
The "marriage gap" is widening, with those struggling financially less likely to tie the knot.

3. The Stork on Strike: The High Cost of Parenthood

The decision to have children is a deeply personal one, but inflation is making it a luxury many can't afford. The gremlin has even infiltrated the nursery, driving up the cost of raising a family.

Childcare Costs Soar: Finding affordable childcare is like searching for a unicorn. Inflation adds fuel to the fire, making it a financial nightmare for parents.
Education: A Pricey Pursuit: From kindergarten to college, the cost of education is a daunting hurdle. Inflation ensures that saving for your child's future is an uphill battle.
Shrinking Families: With less disposable income, families are forced to make tough choices. Delayed parenthood and smaller family sizes are becoming the norm.

Global Trends:

Fertility rates are plummeting worldwide as economic uncertainty casts a shadow over family planning.
The average age of first-time mothers is rising as couples grapple with the financial burden of parenthood.

Conclusion: Reclaiming Our Future

Inflation is a formidable foe, but we cannot let it dictate the course of our lives. We need to fight back, demanding policies that promote affordable housing, accessible childcare, and wages that keep pace with the rising cost of living. Only then can we reclaim our dreams and ensure that the gremlin of inflation doesn't steal our future.

The Gig Economy: A Rollercoaster Ride for Young Minds
The gig economy, a dazzling constellation of temporary jobs and freelance gigs, has emerged as a dominant force in the modern labor market. Fueled by the relentless march of technology and a growing desire for flexible work arrangements, it has become a beacon for young people seeking freedom and autonomy. But beneath the shiny surface lies a precarious reality, one that can take a heavy toll on the mental health of these young adventurers.

Imagine a young graphic designer, fresh out of college, navigating the gig economy maze. One week, she's overflowing with projects, her creativity flowing like a river. The next, she's staring at an empty inbox, anxiety gnawing at her as she wonders where the next paycheck will come from. This "feast or famine" cycle, so characteristic of gig work, can be a psychological minefield.

The Unpredictable Income Rollercoaster:

Stress and Anxiety: The constant uncertainty of income can trigger a chronic state of stress and anxiety. Imagine living with a knot in your stomach, constantly worrying about paying rent or affording groceries. Sleepless nights, headaches, and digestive issues become unwelcome companions.
Depression's Shadow: Financial insecurity can cast a long shadow, leading to feelings of hopelessness and low self-esteem. The relentless

struggle to make ends meet can chip away at one's sense of worth, leaving them vulnerable to depression's grip.
Cognitive Fog: When financial worries loom large, our brains can become overloaded. Decision-making becomes muddled, concentration wavers, and problem-solving abilities suffer. It's like trying to navigate a maze while blindfolded.
Strained Relationships: Financial stress doesn't stay confined to our minds; it spills over into our personal lives. Arguments erupt, resentment simmers, and social withdrawal becomes a tempting escape.

Beyond the Individual:

The mental health impact of the gig economy extends beyond the individual. It ripples through families, communities, and society as a whole. When young people struggle with financial insecurity and mental health challenges, their potential contributions to society are diminished.

Navigating the Turbulence:

So, how can we support young people in this new world of work?

Financial Empowerment: Equipping young people with the knowledge and skills to manage their finances is crucial. Budgeting, saving, and understanding the tax implications of gig work can help them weather the income storms.
Mental Health Support: Access to affordable mental health services is essential. We need to break down the stigma surrounding mental health and ensure that young people have the support they need to navigate the challenges of the gig economy.
Fairer Gig Economy: Advocating for fair labor practices, such as minimum wage guarantees and portable benefits, can help create a more stable and supportive environment for gig workers.
Building Community: Fostering a sense of community among gig workers can combat isolation and provide a much-needed support network. Co-working spaces, online forums, and peer-to-peer mentoring programs can help create a sense of belonging.
The gig economy is here to stay. It's a powerful engine of innovation and flexibility, but it also presents unique challenges. By addressing

the mental health risks associated with precarious employment, we can ensure that the gig economy empowers young people, rather than leaving them stranded on a rollercoaster of uncertainty.

The Joneses are Broke: Why Chasing Inflated Dreams on social media is Making Us Miserable

Forget keeping up with the Joneses. In 2024, the Joneses are probably drowning in credit card debt and secretly sobbing into their avocado toast (which, let's face it, costs a small fortune these days). Thanks to the "inflationary lens," that distorted reality where everyone else seems wildly successful while we're stuck in the financial mud, we're all feeling the pressure.

Social media, that digital carnival of curated perfection, throws gasoline on the fire. We scroll through feeds overflowing with exotic vacations, designer clothes, and impossibly perfect homes, leaving us feeling like we're failing at life's game. But here's the secret: those picture-perfect lives are often just smoke and mirrors, carefully constructed illusions designed to rake in likes and followers.

The truth is, inflation is a sneaky thief, stealing our joy and warping our sense of accomplishment. That promotion you finally got? Eaten up by the rising cost of rent. The new car you saved for? Now a distant dream thanks to soaring gas prices. It's like running on a treadmill – you're working hard, but going nowhere fast.

This constant comparison game, fueled by social media and magnified by inflation, is a recipe for disaster. It's like we're all trapped in a twisted version of "Black Mirror," where our self-worth is measured by the number of likes on our latest post and the size of our bank accounts.

But there's hope. We can break free from this toxic cycle. It starts with ditching the "compare and despair" mentality. Unfollow those accounts that make you feel inadequate, and curate your digital world with content that inspires and uplifts.

Remember, true success isn't about flashing cash or accumulating things. It's about finding joy in the everyday, appreciating what we have, and pursuing goals that truly matter to us. Maybe it's finally writing that novel, learning a new language, or simply spending more time with loved ones.

Let's rewrite the narrative. Instead of chasing inflated dreams on social media, let's focus on building authentic lives filled with genuine connection, personal growth, and a healthy dose of gratitude. After all, happiness isn't about keeping up with the Joneses; it's about discovering what truly makes you feel alive.

Here are a few more ideas to combat the "Inflationary Lens":

Become a financial ninja: Take control of your finances. Create a budget, track your spending, and explore ways to increase your income. Knowledge is power, and understanding your financial situation can reduce anxiety and empower you to make informed decisions.
Embrace the "enough" mentality: We live in a culture that constantly tells us we need more, more, more. Challenge this narrative by focusing on what you already have and appreciating the simple things in life.
Find your tribe: Surround yourself with people who lift you up and support your journey. Genuine connection and shared experiences are far more valuable than any material possession.
Practice self-compassion: Be kind to yourself. We all make mistakes and face challenges. Instead of beating yourself up, treat yourself with the same kindness and understanding you would offer a friend.
Remember, you are not alone in this struggle. By shifting our focus, embracing authenticity, and practicing self-compassion, we can break free from the grip of social comparison and the inflationary lens. Let's create a world where true success is measured not by material wealth, but by the richness of our experiences and the depth of our connections.

The Boomerang Effect: When Generations Collide (and Maybe, Just Maybe, Connect)

The Nest Refilled: Not Empty, just... Different

Remember that feeling of freedom when you finally launched into the world, a fledgling leaving the nest? Imagine the surprise when that fledgling comes back, fully grown, with a suitcase full of laundry and a backpack full of student debt. That's the "boomerang generation" in a nutshell.

Sky-high housing costs, a job market that's tougher than a two-dollar steak, and the ever-looming shadow of student loans – these are just some of the culprits forcing young adults back into their childhood bedrooms. But while multigenerational living can be a lifesaver financially, it can also be a minefield for everyone's mental well-being.

Young Adults: From Independence Back to Dependence?

It's a confusing time. On one hand, there's the comfort of home-cooked meals and the familiar scent of Mom's laundry detergent. On the other, there's the nagging feeling of failure, the frustration of stalled independence, and the awkwardness of curfews when your bedtime routine used to involve Netflix and takeout.

This emotional seesaw can lead to:

The "Groundhog Day" Blues: Waking up in your childhood bedroom can feel like being stuck in a time warp. Depression can creep in, making it hard to see a future beyond these familiar walls.
Anxiety Attacks: The pressure to "figure it out" while feeling like a teenager again can be a recipe for anxiety. Job hunting, finances, relationships – it's a lot to handle when you're also navigating the minefield of family dynamics.
The Self-Esteem Struggle: Returning home can feel like taking a step backward. That inner critic starts whispering, "You're not good enough, independent enough, successful enough."
Identity Crisis 2.0: Just when you thought you were figuring out who you are, bam! You're back in the role of "child," which can make it hard to navigate your identity as an adult.
The Temptation of Escape: For some, the stress can be overwhelming, leading to unhealthy coping mechanisms like substance abuse.

Factors that turn up the heat:

Why are you back? Returning home due to a job loss can hit harder on self-esteem than, say, taking a break between degrees.

How long is this for? A short stay might feel like a vacation. An extended stay? That's when tensions can rise and anxieties fester. How's your relationship with your parents? A strong, supportive bond can be a buffer. A strained relationship? Get ready for some fireworks. How do you cope with stress? Some people thrive in chaos, others crumble. Your coping style plays a huge role in how you navigate this transition.

Parents: From Empty Nest to... Full House (Again!)

Remember all those plans you had for your newfound freedom? The travel brochures, the hobby classes, the quiet evenings? Well, it's time to adjust. Having your adult child move back in can be a whirlwind of emotions.

Here's what parents might experience:

Stress Overload: Finances are often the biggest worry. There's also the added pressure of helping your child navigate their challenges while dealing with your own.
Anxiety Amplified: Concerns about your child's future, your own aging, and the impact on your relationship with your partner can keep you up at night.
Empty Nest Blues (Redux): Just when you were getting used to the quiet, the house is full again. It's normal to grieve the loss of your independence and the life you envisioned.
Resentment Rising: If you feel like your child isn't taking responsibility or is taking advantage, resentment can simmer beneath the surface.

Factors that add fuel to the fire:

Why did they come back? If you feel your child is making poor choices, it can be harder to be supportive.
How long will they stay? A short visit is a joy. An indefinite stay? That requires some serious adjustments.
How's your relationship with your child? A strong bond makes it easier to navigate challenges. A strained relationship? Get ready for some bumps in the road.

How do you handle stress? Are you a cool cucumber or do you tend to explode? Your coping style will influence how you handle this new dynamic.

Finding Harmony: Tips for Navigating Multigenerational Living

Whether you're a boomerang kid or a parent with a refilled nest, here are some tips to make the experience more positive:

For Boomerang Kids:

Take Charge: Actively look for a job, go back to school, or pursue your passions. This shows initiative and gives you a sense of purpose.
Set Boundaries: Talk to your parents about needing personal space and time. This helps avoid feeling suffocated and allows everyone to maintain some independence.
Stay Connected: Don't isolate yourself. Keep in touch with friends and maintain your social life outside the family.
Seek Support: If you're struggling, don't hesitate to talk to a therapist or counselor. It's a safe space to process your emotions and develop coping strategies.

For Parents:

Open Communication is Key: Talk to your child about expectations, boundaries, and finances. Clear communication prevents misunderstandings and resentment.
Be Supportive (But Realistic): Offer emotional support and guidance, but also encourage your child to take responsibility for their own life.
Set Boundaries: Just like your child needs boundaries, so do you. Make sure you have time for yourself and your relationship with your partner.
Prioritize Self-Care: Don't neglect your own well-being. Make sure you're getting enough sleep, eating healthy, exercising, and engaging in activities you enjoy.
Seek Support: If you're feeling overwhelmed, talk to a therapist or counselor. They can help you navigate the challenges and find healthy ways to cope.

The Bottom Line

Multigenerational living can be a rollercoaster ride, full of ups and downs, twists and turns. But with open communication, clear boundaries, and a healthy dose of empathy, it can also be an opportunity to strengthen family bonds and rediscover the meaning of home. It's a chance to rewrite the narrative, not as a story of failure or burden, but as a chapter of resilience, growth, and unexpected connection.

Chapter 2: Unequal Burdens

The Empty Plate: When Hunger Haunts the Mind
Imagine a gnawing emptiness, not just in your stomach, but in your soul. That's the reality for millions struggling with food insecurity, a silent epidemic amplified by the skyrocketing grocery prices of 2024. It's not just about missing meals; it's about the constant, corrosive anxiety that eats away at mental well-being.

A Mind Under Siege

Food insecurity isn't a switch that flips on and off; it's a relentless pressure that keeps the body in "fight-or-flight" mode. Imagine your brain flooded with cortisol, the stress hormone, day in and day out. It's like trying to think clearly in a hurricane.

Sleep becomes a distant memory: Worrying about where the next meal will come from keeps the mind racing, making restful sleep a luxury many can't afford.
Focus blurs, decisions falter: The mental bandwidth needed to simply survive leaves little room for learning, problem-solving, or even just enjoying life.
Social circles shrink: Shame and embarrassment become barriers, isolating individuals and families from the support they desperately need.

The Price We Pay: More Than Dollars and Cents

2024 has been a brutal year. Geopolitical turmoil, supply chain chaos, and climate change have conspired to make basic groceries a luxury good. Those already struggling are pushed to the brink, forced to make impossible choices between food and other essentials.

Empty Stomachs, Empty Souls: The Nutritional Deficit

Our brains are biological machines, and they need the right fuel to function. When essential nutrients are missing, the consequences can be devastating:

Iron: Without it, our brains are starved of oxygen, leading to fatigue, depression, and a feeling of mental fog.
Omega-3s: These healthy fats are like brain food, helping to stabilize mood and keep things running smoothly. A deficiency can feel like the world is constantly off-kilter.
Vitamin D: The "sunshine vitamin" isn't just for strong bones; it's crucial for brain development and function. Low levels can plunge us into darkness, both literally and figuratively.

Faces of Food Insecurity

This crisis has a human face, and it's reflected in the struggles of people like:

Sarah: A single mom forced to skip meals so her kids can eat, her anxiety a constant companion.
Maria: An elderly widow relying on cheap, processed food, her once vibrant mind now clouded by nutritional deficiencies.
David: A college student juggling work and studies, his hunger pangs a distraction from his dreams.

Breaking the Cycle: A Call to Action

This isn't just a problem for individuals to solve; it demands a collective response.

Policymakers: We need stronger safety nets, programs that provide not just food, but also mental health support and nutritional education.
Communities: Food banks, community gardens, and meal delivery services are lifelines for those in need.
Each of Us: Awareness, empathy, and action are our most powerful tools in the fight against food insecurity.
The empty plate is a symbol of a deeper hunger, a hunger for security, for dignity, for a life free from the constant gnawing of worry. It's time to fill those plates, and in doing so, nourish not just bodies, but minds and spirits as well.

      The year is 2024, and the world is in the throes of an inflationary crisis not seen in decades. The cost of living is skyrocketing, making everyday essentials like food, housing, and transportation significantly more expensive. This economic strain is acutely felt by everyone, but it's particularly devastating for those with limited resources who are already struggling to make ends meet. Among those hit hardest are individuals dealing with mental health challenges.

Mental healthcare, even in the best of times, can be expensive and inaccessible. Therapy sessions, medications, and other treatments often come with hefty price tags. When inflation forces individuals to choose between putting food on the table and taking care of their mental health, a heartbreaking trade-off occurs. This trade-off can have dire consequences, exacerbating existing mental health conditions and preventing people from seeking the help they desperately need.

The Real-World Dilemmas

The consequences of inflation-induced trade-offs in mental healthcare are far-reaching and devastating:

Delayed or Forgone Treatment: When faced with rising costs for basic necessities, individuals may postpone or completely forgo mental health treatment. This can lead to a worsening of symptoms, increased risk of hospitalization, and even suicidal ideation.
Medication Non-Compliance: The cost of prescription medications for mental health conditions can be prohibitive. As a result, individuals may skip doses, cut pills in half, or stop taking their medication altogether, leading to a resurgence of symptoms and potential health complications.
Increased Stress and Anxiety: Financial strain is a significant contributor to stress and anxiety. When inflation forces individuals to make difficult choices between basic needs and mental healthcare, it can create a vicious cycle of worsening mental health and financial instability.
Reduced Access to Care: Inflation can also affect the availability of mental health services. As costs rise, providers may be forced to reduce their services, limit their intake of new patients, or even close their practices altogether. This can create further barriers to accessing care, particularly for those in underserved communities.

Examples and Case Studies

The Single Mother: Sarah is a single mother struggling to raise two young children on a limited income. She has been diagnosed with depression and anxiety, but her therapy sessions have become increasingly unaffordable. Faced with the choice between paying for her children's school supplies and continuing therapy, Sarah reluctantly decides to discontinue her treatment. Her mental health deteriorates, making it harder for her to cope with the daily challenges of parenting and making ends meet.

The College Student: Alex is a college student with a part-time job. He has been managing his anxiety with medication and regular therapy sessions. However, with the rising cost of tuition, rent, and food, Alex finds himself unable to afford both his medication and his therapy. He decides to stop taking his medication, hoping that he can manage his anxiety through therapy alone. However, his anxiety worsens, affecting his academic performance and his ability to maintain his job.

The Elderly Couple: John and Mary are a retired couple living on a fixed income. Mary has been diagnosed with Alzheimer's disease, and her medication costs are steadily increasing. As inflation eats away at their savings, John and Mary are forced to make difficult choices about their healthcare. They cut back on their own medications and reduce their spending on groceries to ensure that Mary can continue receiving her Alzheimer's medication.

The Way Forward

The trade-off between basic needs and mental healthcare is a complex issue with no easy solutions. However, there are steps that can be taken to address this growing crisis:

Increase Funding for Mental Health Services: Governments and healthcare organizations need to invest more in mental health services to ensure that they are accessible and affordable for everyone.

Expand Insurance Coverage: Insurance companies should expand their coverage of mental health services and reduce out-of-pocket costs for patients.

Promote Awareness and Reduce Stigma: It is crucial to promote awareness of mental health issues and reduce the stigma associated

with seeking help. This can encourage more people to seek treatment and support.
Address the Root Causes of Inflation: Ultimately, addressing the root causes of inflation is essential to alleviating the financial strain on individuals and families. This may involve implementing policies that stabilize prices, support wage growth, and reduce income inequality. The current inflationary environment is forcing individuals with limited resources to make impossible choices between their basic needs and their mental health. This trade-off has dire consequences, exacerbating existing mental health conditions and preventing people from seeking the help they need.

By taking action to increase funding, expand insurance coverage, promote awareness, and address the root causes of inflation, we can work towards a future where everyone has access to the mental healthcare they deserve.

The "Weathering Hypothesis": When Life's Storms Leave Their Mark

Imagine a weathered old house. It's seen years of harsh sun, relentless rain, and maybe even a few hurricanes. The paint is peeling, the wood is warped, and it just looks...older than its years. That's kind of what happens to people facing constant stress from things like poverty and discrimination. This is the core of the "Weathering Hypothesis."

It's like life throws extra storms at some people, and their bodies just wear down faster. Dr. Arline Geraniums, who came up with this idea, says it's not just about feeling stressed; it's about how that stress gets under your skin and changes you from the inside out.

Stress: The Invisible Thief of Time

Think of your body like a car. A little stress is like a short drive – no big deal. But constant stress is like driving that car non-stop, with the pedal to the metal. Eventually, something's going to give.

This constant wear and tear are called "allostatic load." It's like your body's stress meter is always in the red zone. And just like that overworked car, things start to break down:

Telomeres Fray: These are like the protective caps on your DNA, but stress makes them wear down faster. It's like your body is aging in fast-forward.
Inflammation Simmers: Imagine your body is constantly fighting off an invisible enemy. This low-level inflammation can lead to all sorts of problems like heart disease and cancer.
Genes Get Tweaked: Stress can actually change how your genes work! It's like someone's messing with the control panel of your body, and those changes can even affect your kids.
Immunity Takes a Hit: When you're stressed, your body is too busy putting out fires to fight off germs. This makes you more likely to get sick.
Brain Power Fades: Stress can fog your thinking and even increase your risk of memory problems later in life.

Inflation Adds Fuel to the Fire

Now, imagine trying to keep that old car running when gas prices are sky-high. That's what inflation does to people already struggling. It makes everything harder:

Empty Plates: Food becomes a luxury, and not having enough to eat can really damage your health.
No Place to Call Home: Rising rents can mean losing your home, which adds a whole new layer of stress.
Healthcare Out of Reach: When you can't afford to see a doctor, even small health problems can become big ones.

Real-Life Weathering

This isn't just a theory; we see it happening in real life:

Black mothers and babies: In the U.S., Black women are more likely to have premature babies or babies with health problems. The stress of racism and inequality plays a big role.
Heartbreak and Stroke: Black Americans are more likely to have heart disease and strokes, and weathering is a big part of the puzzle.
Memory Loss: People facing constant stress may experience memory problems and dementia earlier in life.

What Can We Do?

The weathering hypothesis is a wake-up call. It shows us that social problems like poverty and discrimination don't just hurt people's feelings; they hurt their bodies too. We need to fight for a fairer world where everyone has a chance to live a healthy life, free from the constant burden of stress.

This means tackling the root causes of poverty and inequality, making sure everyone has access to good healthcare and affordable housing, and creating a society where everyone feels safe and respected. It's a big challenge, but it's one we need to face if we want to stop the weathering effect and ensure everyone has a chance to age gracefully.

The Heartbeat of Resilience: How Communities Are Rising Together

In a world where challenges seem to multiply by the day, a powerful wave of hope is swelling from the ground up. It's the spirit of community, the unwavering belief that together, we are stronger. This isn't just about survival; it's about weaving a vibrant tapestry of resilience, thread by thread, in the very heart of adversity.

Community Gardens: Where Hope Blooms

Imagine a concrete jungle blossoming with life. Community gardens are more than just patches of green; they're sanctuaries where the seeds of resilience are sown. They're places where fresh food nourishes bodies and shared laughter nourishes souls.

Ron Finley: The Gangster Gardener - Ron Finley, a rebel with a cause, took on the food deserts of South-Central LA with a shovel and a dream. He transformed neglected parkways into edible oases, proving that even in the harshest landscapes, beauty and nourishment can thrive. His "Ron Finley Project" is a testament to the power of one man to ignite a community and cultivate change.

Growing Home: Harvesting Second Chances - In Chicago, the Growing Home Community Garden is not just about growing vegetables; it's about growing people. Formerly incarcerated individuals find new purpose and skills in the soil, transforming their lives while nourishing their community.

Mutual Aid Networks: The Lifeline of Solidarity

When the storms of life hit, mutual aid networks are the safety nets that catch us. They're built on the simple yet profound idea that we're all in this together.

Bed-Stuey Strong: Neighbors Helping Neighbors - When the pandemic struck, the residents of Bed-Stuey, Brooklyn didn't wait for help; they became the help. Bed-Stuey Strong, a grassroots mutual aid network, sprang into action, delivering groceries, providing financial assistance, and proving that even in the midst of isolation, connection and compassion can flourish.

The People's Kitchen Collective: Food is Love - In Oakland, California, The People's Kitchen Collective is serving up more than just meals; they're serving up dignity and hope. Their pay-what-you-can model ensures that everyone has a seat at the table, regardless of their circumstances.

Beyond the Garden Gates: Innovation in Action

Resilience takes many forms, and communities are finding creative ways to empower themselves and build a better future.

Soul Fire Farm: Reclaiming the Roots of Justice - This Afro-Indigenous-centered farm in upstate New York is a beacon of food sovereignty and social justice. They're not just growing food; they're growing a movement, empowering BIPOC communities to reclaim their ancestral connection to the land and build a more equitable food system.

Cooperation Jackson: Building a Solidarity Economy - In Jackson, Mississippi, Cooperation Jackson is proving that another world is possible. They're creating worker-owned cooperatives, building affordable housing, and weaving a tapestry of economic justice that puts power back into the hands of the people.

The Tapestry of Resilience

These stories are just a glimpse into the incredible tapestry of resilience being woven by communities around the world. They remind us that even in the face of overwhelming challenges, the human spirit has an unyielding capacity to adapt, innovate, and create a better future. It's a future where we not only survive, but thrive, together.

Chapter 3: The Gig Economy

The Algorithm and Anxiety

In the heart of the bustling gig economy, where the promise of freedom and flexibility lures workers into a digital labyrinth, a silent battle is being waged on the human psyche. Algorithms, the invisible puppet masters of the platform world, dictate the rhythm of work, leaving individuals tethered to a precarious existence of unpredictable workflows and relentless performance metrics.

Imagine Sarah, a single mother navigating the labyrinth of ride-hailing apps. One moment, her phone buzzes with ride requests, a fleeting hope of a stable income. The next, an eerie silence descends, leaving her stranded in a sea of uncertainty. The algorithm, her ever-watchful boss, holds her fate in its digital hands.

Or picture Alex, a talented writer trapped in the panopticon of online content platforms. Each keystroke is shadowed by the looming presence of performance metrics, an invisible judge scrutinizing every word. The fear of a negative rating haunts his thoughts, casting a long shadow over his creativity.

These are not isolated cases. Across the gig economy, countless individuals are grappling with the mental health consequences of algorithmic management. Unpredictable workflows disrupt the rhythm of life, making it impossible to plan, to dream, to simply breathe. Constant performance monitoring transforms work into a relentless race, where self-worth is measured in stars and ratings.

Social isolation compounds the problem, leaving gig workers stranded on a digital island. The camaraderie of the traditional workplace is replaced by the cold glow of the computer screen, fostering a sense of loneliness and detachment.

The gig economy, once hailed as a beacon of freedom, is slowly revealing its dark side. The promise of autonomy has morphed into a precarious existence, where algorithms reign supreme and human well-being takes a backseat.

It's time to reclaim the human element in the gig economy. To build platforms that prioritize worker well-being, not just profits. To foster a sense of community and support, not just competition and isolation. To create a future where algorithms serve humanity, not the other way around.

This is the human story behind the algorithm and anxiety. A story that demands our attention, our empathy, and our action.

The Cracked Screen of Success: Hustle Culture and the Price of Inflation

Anya stared at her phone, the reflection of her tired eyes staring back from the cracked screen. Another notification. Another "opportunity" to "level up" her side hustle. This one promised a six-figure income in six months, all while working from the beach. Anya scoffed. The beach was currently buried under three feet of snow, and her bank account was looking as barren as the winter landscape outside her window.

Anya was the epitome of the Side-Hustle Superstar. By day, she was a graphic designer for a struggling marketing firm, her creativity stifled by endless revisions and demanding clients. By night (and weekends, and lunch breaks), she poured her soul into her Etsy shop, designing quirky stickers and whimsical prints. It had started as a creative outlet, a way to reclaim some joy in her work. But now, with inflation eating away at her paycheck and the pressure to "monetize her passion" mounting, it felt like just another job.

Across town, Marcus, the Instagram Entrepreneur, was meticulously crafting his next post. A photo of him "working" from a trendy coffee shop, laptop open, a carefully positioned latte beside him. The caption would read something like, "Grind never stops! Building my empire, one sip at a time. #entrepreneur-life #hustle #success-mindset." What the picture wouldn't show was the mounting anxiety churning in his stomach. His "empire" was a drop shipping business selling overpriced phone cases, and his sales were plummeting faster than the stock market during a recession. He was trapped in a cycle of fake it tells you make it, the pressure to maintain the facade crushing him.

Meanwhile, Sarah, the "Fail Fast" Founder, was on her fourth startup in as many years. Her latest venture, an AI-powered pet food dispenser, was burning through cash faster than a hungry Labrador. She'd pitched to countless investors, only to be met with the same refrain: "The market's too volatile. Come back when things stabilize." Inflation had turned venture capitalists into cautious turtles, and Sarah's dream was slowly suffocating under the weight of economic uncertainty.

These are the faces of hustle culture in the age of inflation. The dreamers, the strivers, the ones who bought into the promise of "be your own boss" and "financial freedom." But the reality is far less glamorous. Inflation is a silent thief, stealing not just purchasing power but also hope and mental well-being.

The Weight of the Invisible Backpack

Imagine each worry, each self-doubt, each late-night panic attack as a brick added to an invisible backpack. The Side-Hustle Superstar carries the bricks of client demands, looming deadlines, and the fear of never escaping the 9-to-5 grind. The Instagram Entrepreneur shoulders the bricks of comparison, imposter syndrome, and the constant need to project an image of effortless success. The "Fail Fast" Founder is weighed down by the bricks of investor rejections, market volatility, and the crushing fear of failure.

This invisible backpack grows heavier with each passing day, each news headline about rising prices, each social media post showcasing someone else's seemingly effortless success. It's a burden that can lead to burnout, anxiety, and depression. It's a burden that can crack even the strongest spirit, just like Anya's phone screen.

But what if we could lighten the load?

What if, instead of glorifying the "always-on" mentality, we embraced a more sustainable approach to success? What if, instead of chasing fleeting trends, we focused on building genuine connections and creating value that truly matters?

Imagine a world where:

Mindfulness isn't a luxury but a necessity. Entrepreneurs take time to disconnect, to breathe, to cultivate inner peace amidst the chaos. Community is the currency of success. Instead of cutthroat competition, we foster collaboration and support networks.
Success is measured not just in dollars but in well-being. We value personal growth, creativity, and the pursuit of passions, not just profits. This is not a pipe dream. It's a choice. A choice to redefine success, to prioritize mental health, and to build a more sustainable and fulfilling future for ourselves and for generations to come.

It starts with a single step. Put down the phone. Close the laptop. Take a deep breath. And remember, you are not alone in this journey.

The Gig Economy's Silent Struggle: When Work Freedom Means Social Isolation

The gig economy. It whispers promises of freedom and flexibility, a siren song of working from anywhere, anytime. But beneath the allure of this independent work life lies a hidden cost: the creeping shadow of social isolation.

Imagine this: a freelance writer, bathed in the glow of their laptop screen, words flowing effortlessly. Yet, a profound silence hangs in the air, broken only by the click of keys. No friendly chatter, no shared laughter, no spontaneous brainstorming sessions. Just the hum of the refrigerator and the distant chirp of birds.

This is the reality for many gig workers, especially those working remotely. They're the soloists in the orchestra of work, playing their part beautifully, but missing the harmony that comes from being part of an ensemble.

The Loneliness of the Long-Distance Worker

Traditional workplaces, for all their flaws, offer a built-in community. There's the camaraderie of shared projects, the gossip around the water cooler, the Friday afternoon drinks. These seemingly trivial interactions weave a tapestry of social connection, a sense of belonging that many gig workers crave.

But in the gig economy, the workplace is often a virtual island. Emails and Zoom meetings become the primary mode of communication, efficient but sterile. The casual banter, the shared jokes, the knowing glances – those subtle threads that bind colleagues together – are often lost in the digital ether.

The Mental Health Price Tag

This lack of social connection takes a toll. Studies have shown that gig workers experience higher rates of loneliness, depression, and anxiety compared to their traditionally employed counterparts. It's a heavy price to pay for the freedom to set your own hours and be your own boss.

Think of the ride-sharing driver, navigating the urban maze, passenger after passenger a fleeting face in the rearview mirror. Or the food delivery courier, zipping through traffic, their only interaction a hurried exchange at the doorstep. These are jobs that can feel incredibly isolating, day after day, mile after mile.

Building Bridges in the Digital Age

So, what's the solution? How can we inject some human warmth into the gig economy? It requires a multi-pronged approach:

Gig workers need to be proactive. Join online communities, attend industry events, seek out co-working spaces. Create opportunities for connection, even if it means stepping outside your comfort zone.
Platforms that host gig workers have a responsibility too. They can facilitate online forums, organize meetups, and provide resources on mental health and well-being.
Policymakers need to recognize the unique challenges of the gig economy and ensure that gig workers have access to the same support systems as traditional employees.
The gig economy is here to stay. It's a powerful engine of innovation and flexibility. But we need to find ways to make it more human-centered, to ensure that the pursuit of work freedom doesn't come at

the cost of our mental well-being. Let's build bridges across the digital divide and create a gig economy where everyone feels connected, supported, and valued.

The Gig Economy: A Symphony of Freedom and Struggle

Imagine a world where work is a melody, played on the instrument of your own choosing, at your own tempo. This is the allure of the gig economy, a vibrant tapestry woven with threads of freedom and flexibility. But beneath this enticing surface lies a complex harmony of challenges, where gig workers often find themselves composing a song of struggle.

The Unseen Conductor: Challenges Facing Gig Workers

Like musicians without a conductor, gig workers often navigate a world of precarious employment, their income fluctuating like a capricious rhythm. The absence of traditional benefits leaves them exposed, like a melody stripped of its supporting chords. Misclassification as independent contractors further isolates them, denying them the ensemble of rights enjoyed by traditional employees.

The platforms that connect gig workers with opportunities can wield immense power, like an overbearing maestro dictating every note. This power imbalance can leave workers feeling like mere instruments in a larger composition, their voices muted, their concerns unheard.

And as the gig economy's tempo increases, so too does the pressure on workers' mental health. The isolation, the relentless pursuit of the next gig, the constant uncertainty – it's a symphony of stressors that can leave even the most resilient feeling out of tune.

A Crescendo of Change: Collective Action and Advocacy

But amidst these challenges, a new movement is taking shape. Gig workers, like a chorus finding its voice, are uniting to demand a more harmonious working environment. They are organizing, advocating, and fighting for their rights, their voices rising in a crescendo of change.

From the bustling streets of New York City to the sun-drenched avenues of California, gig workers are forming alliances, like sections of an orchestra coming together to create a richer sound. They are utilizing digital tools to connect and mobilize, their voices echoing through online forums and social media platforms.

They are engaging in direct action, staging protests and strikes that disrupt the gig economy's rhythm, forcing platforms to take notice. They are pursuing legal action, challenging misclassification and unfair labor practices, seeking to rewrite the score of the gig economy.

And they are advocating for policy changes, lobbying for laws that protect their rights and ensure their well-being. They are demanding a system where the music of work is played on a level playing field, where every musician has a voice, and where the melody of freedom is not accompanied by a counterpoint of struggle.

Mental Health: A Countermelody of Support

Recognizing that the gig economy's pressures can take a toll on mental health, workers are also creating spaces for support and healing. Peer support groups offer a place to share experiences and find solace in shared struggles, like a chamber ensemble providing intimate connection.

They are advocating for access to affordable mental health services, ensuring that every gig worker has the resources to maintain their emotional well-being, like a skilled technician tuning an instrument to its optimal pitch.

And they are pushing for workplace policies that promote mental health, demanding that platforms prioritize the well-being of their workers, like a conductor ensuring that the music is played with passion, not pain.

The Final Movement: A Symphony of Hope

The fight for gig worker rights and mental health support is a complex and ongoing symphony. But through collective action, advocacy, and a commitment to mutual support, gig workers are composing a new movement, one that promises a more harmonious future.

They are challenging the status quo, demanding a gig economy where the melody of freedom is played in harmony with the rhythms of fairness, justice, and well-being. It's a symphony of hope, a testament to the power of collective action, and a beacon for a future where work is a source of fulfillment, not just struggle.

Chapter 4: The Anxious Mind

Why That Price Hike Feels Like a Punch in the Gut (and a Tiny Discount Barely Makes Us Blink)

Remember that time you lost a Rs. 500 notes in the bustling Sunday market? The sinking feeling in your stomach, the frustration, the "could've-bought-a-whole-plate-of-puri-with-that" lament. Now, imagine finding that same amount tucked into an old book. Sure, it's nice, but does it evoke the same intensity of emotion? Probably not. That, my friend, is loss aversion whispering in your ear.

We humans are wired weird. Our brains, those magnificent lumps of grey matter, are obsessed with avoiding loss. It's like they've got this internal alarm bell that shrieks bloody murder at the slightest hint of losing something, while a gain gets a polite golf clap at best. Blame it on our ancestors who were constantly dodging saber-toothed tigers and fighting off starvation. Survival meant prioritizing threat avoidance, and that instinct is deeply ingrained in us.

Now, enter inflation, the sneaky thief that silently picks our pockets. Prices creep up, our hard-earned money buys less, and suddenly that dream vacation feels a little further out of reach. It's like being on a treadmill that's slowly increasing its speed – you're running faster and faster, but staying in the same place. And that, my friend, is infuriating.

Loss aversion amplifies the sting of inflation. Every price hike feels like a personal attack, a tiny betrayal by the universe. That extra 10 rupees for your daily commute? It triggers a disproportionate wave of frustration, even if you got a bonus at work last week. Our brains fixate on that loss, ignoring the bigger picture.

This explains why businesses are so hesitant to lower wages, even when times are tough. Imagine the uproar if your boss announced a pay cut, even if it's technically in line with the current economic climate. It feels like a punch in the gut, a loss of hard-earned status.

But here's the kicker: this bias isn't just about money. Remember that amazing dress you snagged on sale? Imagine the store calling a week later, saying they made a mistake and need to charge you full price. Outrageous, right? That's the endowment effect in action – we overvalue things simply because we own them. Selling that dress, even at a profit, feels like a loss.

So, what can we do? First, acknowledge the enemy. Recognize that loss aversion is a powerful force, a primal instinct that influences our decisions. Second, arm yourself with knowledge. Understand how inflation works, how to protect your savings, and how to make smart investments. Don't let fear dictate your choices.

Finally, let's challenge the status quo. Demand transparency from businesses and policymakers. Call out those sneaky "pennies-a-day" subscription tactics that exploit our loss aversion. By understanding our biases, we can make more rational choices and build a more secure future.

After all, we're not just dodging saber-toothed tigers anymore. We're navigating a complex economic landscape, and knowledge is our most powerful weapon.

The Urge to Splurge: How Inflation Makes Us Spend Like There's No Tomorrow

Remember that time you had to have that new gadget, even though your bank account whimpered? Or when you convinced yourself that a weekend getaway was essential for your mental health, despite the looming credit card bill? That's your brain on present bias, my friend. And in times of inflation, this sneaky little bias goes into overdrive, turning us into impulsive spendthrifts.

Present Bias: The "I Want It Now" Gremlin

Imagine your brain as a playground. Present bias is the impatient kid who wants the swing right now, even if it means pushing someone else off. It's the voice that whispers, "Treat yourself! You deserve it!" while conveniently ignoring the long-term consequences.

Inflation: The Sneaky Price-Hiker

Inflation is like that mischievous friend who keeps raising the stakes in a game. Suddenly, your favorite coffee costs an extra dollar, and that dream vacation seems a million miles out of reach. This creates a sense of urgency, a feeling that if you don't buy it now, you might never be able to afford it.

The Perfect Storm: When Present Bias Meets Inflation

When these two forces collide, it's like a shopper's paradise (or a financial disaster waiting to happen). Here's how inflation fuels our "buy now, think later" mentality:

Shrinking Money: Inflation makes your money feel like a melting ice cube. Every day, it loses a little bit of its buying power. So, that fancy dinner tonight seems like a better deal than saving for a rainy day.
The FOMO Frenzy: Remember those concert tickets that sold out in minutes? Inflation creates a fear of missing out (FOMO) on everything. We rush to buy things before they become even more expensive, even if we don't really need them.
The Hedonic Treadmill: We humans are masters of adaptation. As prices rise, we get used to them, and suddenly, that "treat" becomes the new normal. It's a vicious cycle of spending and chasing the next dopamine hit.

Taming the Spending Beast

So, how do we break free from this impulsive spiral? Here are a few tricks:

Budgeting: Your Financial GPS: A budget isn't about deprivation; it's about making conscious choices. It helps you see where your money is going and identify those sneaky "treat yourself" moments that are secretly draining your account.
Goal Setting: Your North Star: Having clear financial goals (a down payment, early retirement, that dream trip) gives you something to strive for. It's like having a map to navigate the choppy waters of inflation.

Delayed Gratification: The Marshmallow Test: Remember that classic experiment where kids were offered one marshmallow now or two later? Practice delaying gratification. Wait a day before making that impulse purchase. You might find you don't even want it anymore. Investing: The Long Game: Investing is like planting a seed that grows over time. It might seem slow at first, but it's the key to building long-term wealth and beating inflation at its own game.

The Bottom Line

Inflation and present bias can be a potent cocktail for financial chaos. But by understanding these forces and adopting smart strategies, we can take control of our spending, achieve our financial goals, and build a future where our money works as hard as we do.

The Whispers of Money: When Secrets and Inflation Tear Love Apart

Imagine love as a garden. It needs sunlight, water, and trust to flourish. But what happens when the weeds of financial infidelity creep in, choking the life out of the relationship?

In a world where prices climb faster than dreams, this hidden betrayal is becoming alarmingly common. It's not just about hiding a credit card bill anymore; it's about the desperation in a partner's eyes as they watch their paycheck shrink while the cost of milk skyrockets.

The Masks We Wear

Financial infidelity isn't a one-size-fits-all monster. It can be the secret side hustle, the online shopping sprees disguised as "groceries," or the hushed phone calls about a mysterious "investment." Each secret digs a deeper hole, burying the truth beneath layers of shame and fear.

Inflation fans the flames of this deception. Suddenly, that little white lie about a new gadget seems justifiable when faced with the crushing weight of rising bills. The pressure to provide, to keep up appearances, can transform even the most honest heart into a master of disguise.

The Scars We Carry

The consequences of financial infidelity are like cracks in a once-solid foundation. Guilt gnaws at the deceiver, while the betrayed partner grapples with a broken trust that can feel impossible to mend. Self-esteem crumbles on both sides, leaving them questioning their worth and the future of their bond.

Stories from the Brokenhearted

Sarah and Mark: He lost his job, the bills piled up, and the shame drove him into the arms of a payday loan shark. Sarah, blindsided by the debt, felt like a stranger in her own home. Their love story, once a source of comfort, became a battlefield of blame and resentment.

Maria and David: She was a freelance writer, her income as unpredictable as the weather. As inflation soared, fear whispered in her ear, convincing her to hide extra earnings in a secret account. When David discovered the truth, it wasn't the money that hurt; it was the realization that the woman he loved had built walls within their own sanctuary.

Healing the Wounds

The road to recovery is paved with honesty, even if it's terrifying. It requires facing the demons of deception and rebuilding trust, brick by fragile brick. Couples therapy can be a lifeline, offering a safe space to unravel the tangled web of secrets and find their way back to each other.

A Shared Journey

Financial infidelity is a storm that threatens to drown even the strongest relationships. But with courage, compassion, and a commitment to transparency, couples can weather the storm and emerge stronger on the other side. Love, after all, is not about perfection; it's about navigating life's challenges hand in hand, even when the path is shrouded in shadows.

Taming Your Financial Gremlins: A Guide to Resilience

We all have them – those pesky financial gremlins that whisper doubts in our ears and make our stomachs churn whenever we glance at our bank accounts. They thrive on uncertainty, whispering anxieties about unpaid bills, unexpected expenses, and that nagging feeling of "never enough."

But here's the secret: you can take those gremlins. Building financial resilience isn't about eliminating anxiety altogether; it's about learning to manage it, to face those fears head-on, and to make sound decisions even when the financial seas get rough.

Meet Maya, the Aspiring Entrepreneur:

Maya, a freelance graphic designer with a passion for sustainable fashion, knows those gremlins all too well. She dreams of launching her own eco-conscious clothing line, but the gremlins love to remind her of her student loan debt and the unpredictable nature of freelance work.

"What if I can't make rent this month?" they hiss. "What if my clients dry up? What if I'm just not cut out for this?"

One rainy Tuesday, as Maya stared at an overdue invoice, she decided she'd had enough. It was time to tame those gremlins and build her financial resilience.

(Insert an illustration here of Maya facing down a small, mischievous gremlin with a dollar sign on its chest)

Understanding the Enemy:

Financial anxiety isn't just a feeling; it's a full-blown physiological response. When those gremlins start whispering, your brain's rational decision-making center takes a backseat, and your emotions take the wheel. This can lead to:

The Ostrich Effect: Burying your head in the sand and avoiding your finances altogether.

Short-Term Tunnel Vision: Focusing only on immediate needs, neglecting long-term goals like saving for retirement or that dream vacation.
Impulsive Decisions: Panic selling investments or making rash purchases driven by fear or a fleeting sense of "retail therapy."
(Insert a playful graphic here depicting the "brain hijack" – perhaps a brain with a tiny gremlin steering wheel)

Taming the Gremlins: Cognitive Strategies

Just like training a puppy, taming your financial gremlins requires consistent effort and the right tools. Here are some strategies to get you started:

Thought Tracking: Keep a "Gremlin Diary" to record your financial anxieties. Notice any patterns? Are there specific triggers that set them off?
Cognitive Restructuring: Challenge those negative thoughts! Ask yourself: "Is this thought really true? What's the evidence? What would I tell a friend in this situation?"
Positive Affirmations: Replace those gremlin whispers with empowering statements. "I am capable of managing my finances. I am making progress towards my goals."
(Insert an interactive element here, like a short quiz: "What's Your Financial Gremlin's Name?")

Building Your Resilience Toolkit:

Cognitive strategies are just one part of the equation. Here are some other tools to add to your arsenal:

Financial Literacy: Knowledge is power! Explore online resources, attend workshops, or even consider a "money book club" with friends.
Tech to the Rescue: Embrace budgeting apps, investment platforms, and online financial planning tools.
Social Support: Talk to trusted friends, family, or a therapist about your financial anxieties. You are not alone!
Mindfulness and Stress Management: Practice deep breathing, meditation, or yoga to calm those gremlins and stay grounded in the present moment.

(Insert a visual here: a toolbox filled with items representing financial literacy, tech tools, social support, and mindfulness practices)

Omar's Journey to Financial Peace:

Omar, a recently widowed father of two, found himself facing a whole new set of financial anxieties after the loss of his wife. He worried about providing for his children, paying the mortgage, and navigating the complexities of his wife's life insurance policy.

Through a support group for widowed parents, Omar discovered the power of shared experiences and learned practical strategies for managing his finances. He started using a budgeting app to track expenses, met with a financial advisor to plan for the future, and found solace in daily mindfulness practices.

(Insert a heartwarming illustration here of Omar and his children, symbolizing hope and resilience)

The Road to Resilience:

Building financial resilience is a journey, not a destination. It's about taking small steps, celebrating victories, and learning from setbacks. Remember, you don't have to conquer those gremlins alone. Reach out for support, embrace your inner strength, and keep moving forward.

Chapter 5: Panic Buying

The Contagion of Fear: How Panic Buying Spreads Like Wildfire

Imagine a bustling city transformed overnight into a ghost town, its streets eerily deserted except for the frantic dash of shoppers raiding supermarket aisles. This isn't a scene from a dystopian novel; it's the stark reality of panic buying, a phenomenon that lays bare the fragility of human behavior in the face of uncertainty.

Like a contagion, fear spreads through communities, whispering anxieties and igniting a primal urge to hoard. Social media, our modern-day town square, amplifies these whispers into a deafening roar. Viral images of empty shelves and frantic shoppers become self-fulfilling prophecies, triggering a domino effect of irrational behavior.

The Digital Bonfire: Social Media's Role in Fanning the Flames

Social media, with its echo chambers and filter bubbles, acts as a potent accelerant. Misinformation and alarmist narratives spread like wildfire, feeding our deepest insecurities. We become trapped in a vortex of fear-mongering, where rational thought takes a backseat to the primal instinct for self-preservation.

Remember the great toilet paper panic of 2020? A simple shortage, fueled by social media frenzy, transformed this mundane household item into a symbol of survival. Images of bare shelves and overflowing shopping carts triggered a global scramble, leaving bewildered shoppers wondering how toilet paper became the new gold standard.

News Outlets: The Unintentional Accomplices

Traditional news outlets, while striving to inform, can inadvertently contribute to the chaos. Sensational headlines and dramatic visuals, designed to capture attention, can amplify anxieties and trigger a cascade of panic buying.

Think of natural disasters, where news reports often focus on the devastation and potential shortages. While these reports serve a vital purpose, they can also spark a rush for essential goods, even when local authorities assure the public that there's no cause for alarm.

The Herd Instinct: When Fear Trumps Logic

Humans are social creatures, hardwired to follow the crowd. In times of crisis, this herd instinct can lead to irrational behavior, as we succumb to the fear of missing out. Panic buying becomes a self-perpetuating cycle, where the fear of scarcity creates the very scarcity, it fears.

The gasoline shortages of the 1970s offers a classic example. A real shortage, exacerbated by panic buying, led to serpentine queues at gas stations and a pervasive sense of desperation. Drivers, fearing they'd be stranded, topped off their tanks even when they were nearly full, creating artificial shortages and fueling the frenzy.

Breaking the Cycle: A Call for Rationality

So, how do we break free from this contagion of fear? How do we cultivate a more resilient society, capable of responding to crises with composure rather than chaos?

Responsible Reporting: News outlets and social media platforms must prioritize balanced reporting, providing context and critical analysis rather than sensationalism.
Government Intervention: Clear and consistent communication from authorities can quell anxieties and prevent the spread of misinformation.
Critical Thinking: We must cultivate media literacy and critical thinking skills, empowering individuals to discern fact from fiction and resist the herd mentality.
Panic buying is a stark reminder of our vulnerability to social influence and the power of fear. By understanding the dynamics of this phenomenon, we can take steps to mitigate its impact and build a more resilient future. Let's choose rationality over reactivity, and ensure that our collective response to crises reflects the best of humanity, not our primal fears.

The Urge to Horde: Why We Lose It Over Potential Shortages

Remember that time everyone went crazy for toilet paper? Or when gasoline lines stretched for miles? We humans have a funny way of reacting to potential shortages – we freak out! It's like our brains go haywire, and suddenly, we're convinced we need a lifetime supply of whatever might become scarce, even if the chances of that happening are slim.

Loss Aversion: The Sting of Missing Out

Imagine losing a $100 bill. Ouch, right? Now imagine finding $100. Feels good, but not as bad as losing it felt, huh? That's loss aversion in action. We hate losing things more than we love gaining them. This fear of missing out plays a big role in how we react to potential shortages.

Zero-Risk Bias: The Comfort of Certainty

We humans crave certainty. We'd rather have a guaranteed, small reward than a chance at a bigger reward with even a tiny risk of getting nothing. This "zero-risk bias" makes us do some pretty irrational things, like paying extra for a "guaranteed" delivery, even if the regular option is almost always on time.

The Shortage Spiral

When these two biases – loss aversion and zero-risk bias – team up during a potential shortage, things can get wild:

Anxiety Overload: The mere thought of not having something we might need sends our anxiety levels through the roof.
Risk Magnification: We start picturing worst-case scenarios, convinced that the shortage will be severe and long-lasting.
The Great Stockpiling Frenzy: Driven by the fear of missing out, we rush to the stores and buy everything in sight, leading to actual shortages and a self-fulfilling prophecy.
Price Explosions: Sellers, seeing the desperation, jack up prices, making essential goods even harder to get.

Social Chaos: In extreme cases, shortages can spark arguments, fights, and even riots as people compete for limited resources.

Taming the Shortage Panic

While these biases are hardwired into us, we can learn to manage them:

Truth and Transparency: Clear, honest information about the shortage can calm nerves and prevent overreactions.
Fair Play: Rationing systems can ensure everyone gets a fair share, preventing hoarding and chaos.
Price Protection: Measures to prevent price gouging can keep essential goods affordable.
Thinking Ahead: Investing in alternative sources and diversifying production can make us less vulnerable to future shortages.

In Conclusion

Loss aversion and zero-risk bias are like those annoying inner voices that make us do silly things when faced with potential shortages. But by understanding these biases, we can make smarter choices, avoid unnecessary panic, and build a more resilient society. After all, we're all in this together, and sharing is caring, especially when resources are scarce.

Panic buying! Just the phrase conjures images of frantic shoppers, empty shelves, and that one guy hoarding all the toilet paper. But there's more to this phenomenon than meets the eye. It's a global dance of fear, uncertainty, and good old-fashioned herd mentality, played out across cultures and centuries.

Remember the Dutch losing their minds over tulips in the 17th century? Tulip Mania! One bulb cost more than a house. Fast forward to the COVID-19 pandemic, and it was toilet paper reigning supreme. From Australia to Venezuela, people were stocking up like the apocalypse was next door.

But why do we do it? Well, fear is a powerful motivator. A sprinkle of uncertainty, a dash of "everyone else is doing it," and bam! You've got a recipe for a shopping frenzy. Our brains are wired to avoid loss, so we overcompensate, just in case.

The consequences? Shortages, price gouging, and a whole lot of stress. It's not a pretty picture. But there's hope! Clear communication, smooth supply chains, and a bit of community love can work wonders.

So, next time you see a crowd swarming the supermarket, take a deep breath. Remember the tulips, remember the toilet paper, and maybe just grab a bag of chips instead. Panic buying? Nah, we're smarter than that.

The Whisper of the Herd: Taming the Panic Buying Beast

Imagine a flock of startled birds, taking flight in a frenzy at the slightest disturbance. That's panic buying in a nutshell – a sudden, irrational surge of consumer behavior driven by fear and the primal instinct to survive. It's like a collective fever dream where toilet paper becomes gold dust and hand sanitizer is the elixir of life.

But what if we could whisper logic into the wind, gently guiding the flock towards calmer skies? That's the power of behavioral interventions, or "nudges," as we like to call them. These subtle cues, grounded in the quirks of human psychology, can steer us away from the precipice of panic and towards more rational choices.

Decoding the Panic Button:

Before we start nudging, let's peek inside the human mind during a panic buying episode. It's not a pretty sight:

The Amygdala's Alarm Bells: Our brain's fear center goes haywire, triggering a fight-or-flight response that makes us hoard resources like squirrels preparing for an endless winter.
The Contagion Effect: Panic buying is like a yawn – incredibly contagious. Seeing empty shelves triggers a primal "fear of missing out" (FOMO), turning us into mindless copycats.
Cognitive Quirks: Our brains are riddled with biases that amplify panic:

Availability Heuristic: We overestimate the likelihood of events that are easily recalled, like that viral video of a brawl over the last bag of flour.

Anchoring Bias: Seeing a "limit 2 per customer" sign screams scarcity, even if the warehouse is overflowing.

Loss Aversion: The agony of running out of diapers outweighs the logic of not needing a year's supply.

Whispering Sanity: A Nudge in the Right Direction

Armed with this knowledge, we can craft clever nudges to counter the panic:

The Art of Calm Communication:
Truth Serum: Drown the rumor mill in a flood of accurate, timely information. Think clear infographics, concise social media updates, and trusted experts debunking myths like digital superheroes.
Abundance is Key: Instead of fueling scarcity fears, emphasize the resilience of the supply chain. "There's enough for everyone, just breathe and buy what you need."
The Messenger Matters: Enlist the voices of calm – doctors, scientists, community leaders – to deliver messages of reason and reassurance.
Preemptive Strikes:
Strategic Stockpiles: Imagine governments and businesses as wise squirrels, creating hidden caches of essential goods to weather any storm.
Supply Chain Jenga: Diversifying supply chains is like playing Jenga with extra blocks – removing one won't bring the whole tower crashing down.
Smooth Operator: Spread out demand with clever tactics like off-peak discounts or designated shopping days based on your astrological sign (why not?).
Limits and Norms: Gently enforce purchase limits to prevent hoarding and ensure everyone gets a slice of the pie.

The Nudge Arsenal:
Framing Frenzy: Present information in a way that encourages cooperation and rational thought. "Be a hero, buy responsibly!"

Default to Zen: Make responsible behavior the easy choice. Online stores can pre-set reasonable purchase quantities, saving us from our impulsive selves.

The Power of the Herd (for Good): Highlight that most people are behaving responsibly, tapping into our innate desire to conform.

Commitment is Key: Encourage public pledges or social media campaigns where people commit to shopping with sanity.

Real-World Magic:

Taiwan's Mask Marvel: During the pandemic, Taiwan's ingenious mask rationing system, using their national health insurance database, ensured everyone had access to this precious commodity.

Germany's Cool Under Pressure: Despite energy concerns during the Ukraine war, Germany kept calm and carried on, thanks to clear communication and a strong sense of community.

Iceland's Volcanic Victory: When a volcano erupted in 2023, Iceland's swift action and proactive communication prevented panic buying, proving that cool heads prevail.

The Future of Nudging:

In an increasingly interconnected world, where disruptions are the new normal, mastering the art of the nudge is crucial. By understanding the human mind and harnessing the power of behavioral science, we can build more resilient communities and create a world where panic buying becomes a relic of the past.

Let's whisper sanity into the chaos, and together, we can take the panic buying beast.

Chapter 6: The Scarcity Trap

The Mind's Tightrope: When Scarcity Makes Us Fall
Imagine your mind as a tightrope walker. Each thought, each decision, each worry is a step across the high wire. Now imagine someone piling weights onto the walker – a bill here, a deadline there, the gnawing fear of not having enough. This is the "cognitive bandwidth tax" of scarcity, where the weight of our worries makes it harder and harder to stay balanced, to make the right steps, to even see the other side.

A Hungry Mind Can't Focus

Think of your brain like a smartphone. Too many apps running, and the battery drains fast, everything slows down. Financial anxieties are like power-hungry apps, constantly draining your mental battery. Suddenly, remembering where you put your keys (working memory) feels like an impossible task. Focusing on a report at work becomes a Herculean effort as worries about rent creep in. It's like trying to read a book in a noisy room – the words are there, but the meaning gets lost in the din.

This isn't just a feeling. In 2024, researchers actually saw this happening. Brain scans of people struggling financially showed weaker activity in the areas responsible for focus and decision-making. It's like their mental "bandwidth" was being used up just to keep worrying, leaving little room for anything else.

Scarcity's Tunnel Vision

Imagine you're lost in a dark forest. Your only light is a narrow flashlight beam. You can only see what's right in front of you – a fallen tree, a patch of thorns. You can't see the path, the way out. This is what scarcity does to our thinking. We become so fixated on the immediate crisis – the overdue bill, the empty fridge – that we lose sight of the bigger picture.

This "tunnel vision" can lead to disastrous choices. Think of the single mom, desperate to feed her kids, who takes out a payday loan with sky-high interest rates. In the short term, it solves the immediate problem. But in the long run, it digs her deeper into the hole, the interest piling up like a mountain.

The Emotional Earthquake

Scarcity doesn't just mess with our minds; it shakes our emotional foundations. Chronic financial stress is like living with a constant earthquake. The ground is never stable, and you're always bracing for the next tremor. This constant state of anxiety can trigger a cascade of emotional problems.

Imagine a couple constantly fighting about money. The tension is thick enough to cut with a knife. Resentment builds, communication breaks down, and suddenly, they're not just facing a financial crisis, but a relationship crisis too. This emotional turmoil further depletes their mental resources, making it even harder to climb out of the financial hole.

Breaking the Cycle, Finding the Light

The good news is that we're not helpless against this "cognitive bandwidth tax." It's like learning to walk the tightrope with those weights still attached. It takes practice, skill, and the right tools.

Financial Literacy: Imagine giving our tightrope walker a balancing pole. That's what financial literacy does. It equips people with the knowledge and skills to navigate their finances, to make informed decisions, and to feel more in control.
Mental Health Support: Sometimes, the weight is just too heavy to bear alone. A therapist can be like a safety net, providing support and strategies to manage the emotional burden of scarcity.
Social Safety Nets: Think of these as strong hands reaching out to steady the tightrope walker. Government programs and community initiatives can provide crucial support, alleviating some of the immediate pressure and giving people a chance to regain their balance.
Mindfulness and Stress Reduction: These are like strengthening the tightrope walker's core, improving their focus and resilience. Techniques like meditation can help calm the mental storm, allowing clearer thinking and better decision-making.

The "cognitive bandwidth tax" of scarcity is a heavy burden, but it's not insurmountable. By empowering individuals, providing support, and strengthening our social safety nets, we can help people walk that tightrope with greater confidence, resilience, and hope.

The Invisible Hand That Squeezes: How Inflation Forces Us to Choose Between Life's Essentials

Imagine life as a vibrant tapestry, woven with threads of education, leisure, health, and savings. Now, picture inflation as an invisible hand slowly tightening around that tapestry, squeezing the joy and vibrancy out of it. This is the stark reality of "tunneling," a phenomenon where rising prices force us to make agonizing trade-offs, sacrificing crucial aspects of our lives just to stay afloat.

The Crushing Weight of "Either/Or"

Inflation isn't just about numbers; it's about the human stories behind those numbers. It's the single mother skipping meals to ensure her child has enough, the elderly couple choosing between heating and medication, the student drowning in debt while chasing their dreams. These are the faces of tunneling, where "both/and" becomes a luxury and "either/or" a harsh reality.

The Dinner Table Dilemma: Do we nourish our bodies with quality food or prioritize essential doctor's visits?
The Roof Over Our Heads vs. Reaching for the Stars: Do we settle for cramped living conditions or invest in our children's education, their passport to a brighter future?
The Gas Tank vs. The Piggy Bank: Do we fill up the car to get to work or save for a rainy day, a safety net against life's uncertainties?
Moments of Joy vs. The Bare Necessities: Do we allow ourselves the occasional movie night or tighten the belt further, sacrificing leisure for survival?

Real-Life Tales of Tunneling

The Working Poor: Imagine working tirelessly, yet still finding yourself trapped in a cycle of scarcity. Inflation becomes an

unforgiving taskmaster, demanding more hours, more sacrifices, and leaving little room for anything but exhaustion.
Single-Parent Heroes: These warriors often bear the brunt of inflation, juggling multiple roles and making impossible choices. Their own well-being takes a backseat as they strive to shield their children from the storm.
Golden Years, Tarnished by Rising Costs: For those on fixed incomes, inflation is a thief, stealing the golden years they worked so hard for. Medications become a luxury, and even basic necessities feel out of reach.
Students, Burdened by Debt and Dreams: The pursuit of knowledge shouldn't come with a crushing weight of debt. Yet, inflation forces many students to choose between their education and their financial future.

The Ripple Effects of Tunneling

The consequences of tunneling extend far beyond individual struggles. It's a societal crisis in the making:

A Widening Gap: Inflation acts as a magnifying glass, amplifying existing inequalities. The vulnerable become more vulnerable, and the dream of upward mobility feels like a distant mirage.
Economic Stagnation: When families prioritize survival over spending, the economy sputters. Businesses suffer, jobs are lost, and the cycle of hardship continues.
Seeds of Social Unrest: As people struggle to make ends meet, frustration simmers. The social fabric weakens, and the foundation of stability begins to crack.

A Call for Empathy and Action

Tunneling is a stark reminder that inflation isn't just an economic issue; it's a human issue. It's a call for empathy, for policies that protect the vulnerable, and for a society that values the well-being of all its members. It's a reminder that we're all interconnected, and that the choices forced upon individuals by inflation ultimately shape the future we all share.

The Scarcity Trap: How Feeling Poor Makes Us Act Poor

Imagine your brain as a computer. When you're constantly worried about money, time, or even love, it's like your computer's RAM is being eaten up by a program called "Scarcity." This program hogs all your processing power, leaving little room for anything else.

This is the scarcity mindset. It's not just about being poor; it's about feeling poor. It's that nagging sense of lack that makes you focus on what you don't have, instead of what you do.

Why Scarcity Makes Us Selfish and Suspicious

Think of a hungry person at a buffet. They might pile their plate high, worried there won't be enough. That's scarcity in action. It makes us:

See the world as a pie: If someone else gets a bigger slice, it means less for us. This "zero-sum" thinking fuels competition and conflict.
Hoard our resources: We become fiercely protective of what we have, whether it's money, time, or even our personal space. Sharing feels like losing.
Build walls, not bridges: We become suspicious of others, especially those we see as different. We fear they'll take what little we have.

Scarcity in the Real World

Job hunting: Ever felt that knot in your stomach when competing for a job? That's scarcity making you see other applicants as enemies, not potential allies.
Fighting over scraps: Whether it's water in a drought-stricken region or the last slice of pizza, scarcity can turn us against each other.
Social unrest: When people feel economically squeezed, they're more likely to take to the streets. Think of the Arab Spring uprisings, fueled by a sense of deprivation.

The Crumbling of Trust

Scarcity doesn't just make us fight; it makes us lose faith in each other.

Cooperation goes out the window: When we're focused on our own needs, we're less likely to lend a helping hand. Community spirit withers.
Suspicion takes root: We start seeing threats everywhere, assuming the worst of others. This can lead to social isolation and paranoia.
Society fractures: As trust breaks down, we retreat into our own groups, creating a divided and fragmented society.

Examples of Scarcity's Toll

The Tragedy of the Commons: Remember that time everyone in your dorm overused the shared kitchen, and it ended up a disaster? That's scarcity leading to the ruin of a shared resource.
The rise of "us vs. them": Scarcity fuels populist movements that prey on fear and division, pitting groups against each other.
The pandemic effect: Remember the toilet paper shortages? COVID-19 created a sense of scarcity that amplified anxiety and hoarding behavior.

Breaking Free from the Scarcity Trap

So, how do we escape this vicious cycle?

Create abundance: Invest in education, infrastructure, and social programs that empower people.
Foster collaboration: Encourage teamwork and community building. Remind people that we're all in this together.
Fight inequality: Reduce economic disparities to create a more level playing field.
Build a shared identity: Celebrate diversity and promote cultural events that bring people together.

The Bottom Line

The scarcity mindset is a thief. It steals our joy, our peace of mind, and our ability to connect with others. By understanding its power and taking steps to counter it, we can build a world where everyone feels like they have enough.

Imagine a World Where "Enough" is Always Enough: Unleashing Your Inner Abundance

Forget the myth of scarcity – it's a story whispered by fear, a phantom that thrives in the shadows of our minds. What if, instead of clinging to lack, we embraced the radical idea that there's enough for everyone? This isn't about wishful thinking, it's about rewiring your reality, cultivating an abundance mindset that transforms not just your bank account, but your entire life.

Think of it like this: scarcity is a cramped, dusty attic, filled with anxieties about what you don't have. Abundance? That's a sun-drenched meadow, bursting with possibilities and the joyful sharing of resources.

Escaping the Scarcity Trap

The scarcity mindset is a master of disguise. It whispers doubts, fuels comparisons, and convinces you that every resource is a zero-sum game. Recognize these sneaky tactics?

Hoarding: Clinging to possessions, time, or even knowledge like a dragon guarding its gold.
Lack-Focused Lens: Constantly scanning for what's missing, blind to the blessings already present.
Success Envy: Seeing others' achievements as a threat, diminishing your own potential.
Decision Paralysis: Fearful of making the "wrong" choice, convinced opportunities are limited.

Stepping into the Abundance Oasis

Now, imagine stepping out of that cramped attic and into the open field of abundance. Here, generosity isn't a loss, it's an investment. Appreciation isn't naive, it's a superpower. And collaboration? It's the key to unlocking exponential growth.

Here's how to cultivate your own abundance garden:

Challenge Your Inner Critic: Those limiting beliefs? Time to weed them out! Replace "I can't afford it" with "How can I create this?"
Gratitude is Your Fertilizer: Daily doses of appreciation nourish your abundance mindset. Keep a gratitude journal, whisper thanks to the universe, savor every sunrise.
Solution-Oriented Vision: Ditch the problem-focused lens. Challenges? They're opportunities in disguise, invitations to innovate and grow.
Visualize Your Abundance Harvest: Close your eyes, and paint a vibrant picture of your ideal life. Feel the joy, the freedom, the boundless possibilities.

Beyond Material Wealth: Abundance in All Areas

Abundance isn't just about overflowing bank accounts. It's about:

Time Abundance: Feeling spacious and present, not constantly rushed and overwhelmed.
Relationship Abundance: Deep, meaningful connections that nourish your soul.
Creativity Abundance: Ideas flowing freely, inspiration striking like lightning.
Health Abundance: Vibrant energy, restful sleep, and a body that feels alive.

Real-World Abundant Souls:

Oprah Winfrey: Rose from poverty and abuse, fueled by an unshakeable belief in her potential and gratitude for every opportunity.
Arianna Huffington: Transformed burnout into a global movement for well-being, proving that success doesn't have to come at the cost of your health.

The Ripple Effect of Abundance

When you embrace abundance, it's not just your life that transforms. You become a beacon of generosity, inspiring others to step into their own power. Imagine a world where everyone believes in "enough."

That's the true magic of abundance – it's contagious, creating a ripple effect of prosperity, joy, and lasting well-being for all.

Ready to unleash your inner abundance and rewrite your reality? The journey starts now.

Chapter 7: Resilience in the Storm

The Power of Social Connection: Building Support Networks and Community Resilience

In our modern world, we're constantly bombarded with information and stimulation, yet many of us feel more isolated than ever. It's like living in a crowded room, but still feeling utterly alone. But there's hope! Strong social ties and active community engagement aren't just nice-to-haves, they're essential ingredients for a fulfilling life, individual well-being, and the resilience of our communities. Let's dive into the incredible power of human connection and explore how it can transform our lives and our world.

Social Ties: Our Lifeline in a Turbulent World

Think of social connections as a safety net that catches us when we stumble. These connections, ranging from our closest confidants to casual acquaintances, provide a buffer against life's inevitable challenges, helping us bounce back stronger and promoting both mental and physical health.

Longer Lives: Research has consistently shown that strong social relationships are linked to a longer lifespan. The impact is comparable to quitting smoking and even surpasses the benefits of regular exercise or maintaining a healthy weight. It's like having a superpower that protects us from the inside out.

Mental Health Boost: Social connections are a potent antidote to loneliness, depression, and anxiety. Feeling loved, supported, and understood can help us weather the storms of life and emerge stronger on the other side.

Physical Health Perks: The benefits of social connection extend beyond our minds. Studies have shown that socially connected individuals have lower rates of cardiovascular disease, stroke, and even dementia. It's like having a team of cheerleaders supporting our physical health.

Coping with Challenges: Life throws curveballs, but social connections equip us with the emotional and practical support needed to navigate those challenges. It's like having a toolbox filled with coping mechanisms, ready to tackle any obstacle.

Community Engagement: Building a Resilient Future Together

Beyond individual well-being, social connections form the bedrock of strong, resilient communities. When we actively engage with our communities, we contribute to a collective ability to withstand and recover from adversity.

Sharing is Caring: Communities provide a platform for sharing resources, knowledge, and support, especially during times of crisis. It's like having a safety net for the entire community.

Collective Power: A sense of community fosters collective efficacy, the belief that we can create positive change together. It's like a ripple effect, where individual actions create waves of change throughout the community.

Social Capital: Community engagement builds social capital, the networks of relationships and trust that facilitate cooperation and mutual benefit. It's like a shared bank account of trust and goodwill that benefits everyone in the community.

Cultural Preservation: Communities play a vital role in preserving cultural heritage and traditions. It's like passing the torch of our cultural legacy to future generations.

Real-World Examples: The Power of Connection in Action

Men's Sheds: These community spaces provide men with a place to connect, share skills, and build social support networks. It's like a clubhouse where men can be themselves and forge meaningful connections.

Community Gardens: These green oases not only provide access to fresh produce but also foster social connections and a sense of belonging. It's like growing a community, one seed at a time.

The Village Movement: This movement empowers older adults to age in place by creating supportive communities. It's like a neighborhood watch program, but for seniors.

Repair Cafés: These community events bring people together to repair broken household items, reducing waste and fostering social interaction. It's like a DIY workshop with a social twist.

Conclusion: The Power of Human Connection

The evidence is clear: social connections and community engagement aren't just optional extras, they're essential ingredients for a healthy and resilient society. Investing in these connections, both individually and collectively, is an investment in our well-being, our communities, and our future. As we navigate the complexities of the 21st century, the power of human connection will continue to be our greatest asset. It's time to embrace the power of connection and build a brighter future together.

Unwind Your Mind: A Journey to Inner Peace in a Chaotic World

Imagine your mind as a bustling city square, filled with noisy thoughts jostling for attention. Stress and anxiety are like unwelcome guests, honking their horns and disrupting the flow. But what if you could transform that chaotic square into a tranquil oasis? That's the power of mindfulness and stress reduction.

Mindfulness: Pressing Pause on the Autopilot

In our whirlwind lives, we often operate on autopilot, rushing from one task to the next without truly experiencing the present moment. Mindfulness is like hitting the pause button, allowing us to step off the treadmill and savor the scenery of our inner world. It's about paying attention to our thoughts, feelings, and sensations without judgment, like a curious observer watching clouds drift by.

Think of it as tuning in to your own internal radio station. Instead of getting swept away by the blaring news of worries and regrets, you can choose to focus on the soothing melody of your breath or the gentle rhythm of your heartbeat.

The Gifts of Presence

The benefits of mindfulness are like precious gems waiting to be discovered:

Stress and Anxiety Melt Away: Like a warm bath for your mind, mindfulness helps soothe the frayed edges of your nervous system.
Focus Sharpens: Imagine a spotlight illuminating your thoughts, allowing you to concentrate with laser-like precision.
Emotions Find Balance: Mindfulness helps you ride the waves of your emotions without getting capsized by them.
Self-Awareness Blossoms: Like a mirror reflecting your inner landscape, mindfulness reveals your true self.
Sleep Becomes a Sanctuary: Quiet the mental chatter and drift off to dreamland with ease.
Resilience Grows Strong: Like a sturdy tree weathering a storm, mindfulness helps you bounce back from life's challenges.

Mindfulness in Action: A Toolkit for Everyday Life

Mindful Breathing: Become an explorer of your own breath, noticing its subtle nuances as it flows in and out.
Body Scan Meditation: Embark on an inner journey, mapping the sensations of your body from toes to head.
Mindful Walking: Transform an ordinary stroll into a sensory adventure, attuning to the rhythm of your steps and the world around you.
Mindful Eating: Savor each bite as a gourmet experience, appreciating the flavors, textures, and aromas of your food.

Meditation: A Deep Dive into Stillness

Meditation is like diving into the depths of a calm ocean, leaving the surface waves of thoughts behind. It's a practice of focusing your mind on a single point, like your breath, a mantra, or an image, creating a sanctuary of stillness within.

Stress Management: A Symphony of Techniques

Beyond mindfulness and meditation, a whole orchestra of stress management techniques awaits:

Progressive Muscle Relaxation: Release tension like a sculptor chiseling away at a block of marble.
Deep Breathing Exercises: Calm the storm within with the soothing rhythm of your breath.
Yoga and Tai Chi: Flow through graceful movements, harmonizing body and mind.
Nature's Embrace: Immerse yourself in the healing power of the natural world.
Journaling: Unburden your thoughts and emotions onto the page, creating space for clarity.

Real-Life Transformations: Stories of Mindfulness in Action

Chronic Pain Finds Relief: Imagine individuals finding solace from persistent pain through the power of mindful awareness.
Anxiety and Depression Ease Their Grip: Witness the transformative effects of mindfulness as it helps people navigate the challenges of mental health.
Workplace Wellbeing Flourishes: Envision a workplace where mindfulness empowers employees to thrive amidst the demands of their jobs.

Embrace the Journey to Inner Peace

Mindfulness and stress reduction are not just techniques; they are pathways to a more fulfilling life. By weaving these practices into your daily routine, you can cultivate a garden of inner peace, where tranquility blossoms even amidst the chaos of the world.

Remember: This is just the beginning of your exploration. Seek guidance from qualified professionals if you're facing significant challenges. May your journey towards well-being be filled with self-discovery and serenity.

Financial Freedom: Your Journey to Inner Peace and Prosperity

Imagine a life where money is no longer a source of stress, but a tool to unlock your dreams. This is the power of financial literacy. It's about understanding your relationship with money and transforming it from a source of anxiety into a source of empowerment.

Budgeting: Painting a Masterpiece with Your Finances

Think of your budget as a canvas, and your income as the colors. Budgeting isn't about restriction; it's about creating a beautiful picture of your financial life.

Know Your Palette: Before you start painting, you need to know your colors. List out all your income sources – your salary, side hustles, even that occasional lucky lottery ticket! Then, identify your expenses. These are the strokes that shape your financial picture.
Sketching Your Vision: Now, imagine the masterpiece you want to create. Do you envision a cozy home, exciting travels, or early retirement? These are your financial goals, and your budget is the roadmap to get there.
Choosing Your Style: Will you use the bold strokes of the 50/30/20 rule, the detailed precision of a zero-based budget, or the tactile feel of the envelope system? Find the budgeting style that speaks to your soul.
Adding the Finishing Touches: Like any masterpiece, your budget needs constant refinement. Review it regularly, adjust your strokes as life throws you curveballs, and watch your financial picture come to life.

Saving: Planting Seeds for a Bountiful Harvest

Saving is like planting seeds for your future. Each dollar you save is a seed that has the potential to grow into something magnificent.

Dream Big: What are the fruits you long to harvest? A down payment on your dream home? A comfortable retirement? Define your financial goals, both big and small.

Prepare for Storms: Life can be unpredictable, like a sudden storm that threatens your garden. An emergency fund is your shelter, protecting you from financial hardship during unexpected events.
Nurture Your Garden: Explore different savings options, like high-yield savings accounts or CDs, to help your seeds grow faster.
Let the Rain Do Its Work: Automate your savings with regular transfers, like setting up a recurring "financial rain shower" to nourish your financial garden.

Making Informed Decisions: Navigating the Financial Jungle

The world of finance can feel like a dense jungle, full of confusing products and hidden dangers. But with the compass of financial literacy, you can confidently navigate this terrain.

Identify the Wildlife: Understand the different creatures inhabiting this jungle – from the docile checking account to the more complex investment options.
Chart Your Course: Assess your risk tolerance. Are you a daring explorer, ready to swing through the trees of high-risk investments, or a cautious trekker, preferring the safer paths?
Seek Guidance from the Locals: Don't be afraid to ask for help. Financial advisors are like experienced guides who can help you navigate the jungle and avoid pitfalls.

Taming the Anxiety Beast: Finding Inner Peace

Financial anxiety can be a ferocious beast, lurking in the shadows and stealing your peace of mind. But with the tools of financial literacy, you can take this beast.

Shine a Light: Understanding your finances is like shining a light into the darkness, dispelling fear and uncertainty.
Build Your Fortress: A solid financial foundation, built on budgeting and saving, is your fortress against the attacks of financial anxiety.
Celebrate Your Victories: Each step you take towards financial literacy is a victory. Celebrate your progress, no matter how small, and acknowledge your growing mastery over your finances.
Conclusion: Embrace the Journey

Financial literacy is not a destination; it's an ongoing journey of learning, growing, and evolving. Embrace this journey with curiosity and courage. Seek knowledge, adapt to change, and celebrate your successes along the way. Remember, financial freedom is not just about numbers; it's about living a life of purpose, peace, and prosperity.

The Power of We: Rising Together to Weather Economic Storms and Protect Our Mental Wellbeing

Imagine a tapestry woven from individual threads, each representing a person grappling with the mental strain of economic hardship. While each thread may seem fragile on its own, when interwoven with others, they form a resilient fabric capable of withstanding immense pressure. This is the power of collective action – the understanding that we are not alone in our struggles and that by joining forces, we can create a safety net that supports us all.

Economic hardship can feel like a silent earthquake, shaking the foundations of our lives and leaving us feeling vulnerable and isolated. The stress of job loss, financial insecurity, and the constant struggle to make ends meet can take a heavy toll on our mental wellbeing. It's like carrying a hidden weight that grows heavier with each passing day, leading to anxiety, depression, and a sense of hopelessness.

But amidst the darkness, there is hope. We are not passive victims of circumstance. We have the power to rewrite the narrative, to transform our individual struggles into a collective force for change. Think of it as a symphony, where each instrument plays a unique part, yet together they create a harmonious melody that resonates with power and beauty.

Here's how we can orchestrate this symphony of change:

Ignite the Spark of Grassroots Movements: Imagine neighbors gathering in a local park, sharing their stories, and brainstorming solutions. This is the essence of grassroots organizing – the power of communities coming together to identify challenges and advocate for change. These movements are the lifeblood of social change, the beating heart of a community determined to create a better future.

Become Architects of Policy: Just as an architect designs a building to withstand the elements, we can become architects of policies that protect our mental health during economic storms. By engaging with elected officials, lobbying for increased mental health funding, and demanding access to affordable care, we can build a society that prioritizes wellbeing.

Unleash the Ripple Effect of Awareness: Imagine a single stone cast into a still pond, creating ripples that spread far and wide. This is the power of public awareness campaigns. By sharing our stories, challenging stigma, and educating others about the link between economic hardship and mental health, we can create a ripple effect that transforms attitudes and inspires action.

Build Sanctuaries of Support: Imagine a community garden where people come together to plant seeds of hope and nurture each other's growth. This is the essence of community-based initiatives. By creating support groups, offering peer counseling, and providing access to resources, we can build sanctuaries of support that offer refuge during difficult times.

Remember the inspiring stories of collective action:

The Mental Health Parity and Addiction Equity Act (MHPAEA): This landmark legislation, achieved through years of tireless advocacy, ensures that mental health is treated with the same importance as physical health. It's a testament to the power of collective voices demanding change.

The "Time to Change" Campaign: This campaign, like a gentle breeze sweeping through society, has challenged the stigma surrounding mental health, creating a more open and accepting environment.

Here's how you can join the movement:

Become an Informed Advocate: Knowledge is power. Educate yourself about the mental health challenges in your community and the policies that impact access to care.

Find Your Tribe: Connect with local organizations, support groups, or online communities dedicated to mental health advocacy. Remember, you are not alone.

Amplify Your Voice: Contact your elected officials, share your story, and demand change. Use social media to spread awareness and mobilize support.

Nurture Your Community: Volunteer your time or donate to organizations providing mental health services. Every act of kindness, no matter how small, contributes to a stronger, more compassionate community.

By embracing the power of collective action, we can transform economic hardship from a source of isolation and despair into a catalyst for positive change. Let us rise together, like a chorus of voices demanding a world where mental wellbeing is valued, protected, and nurtured, no matter the economic climate.

Chapter 8: Community as Antidote

Mutual Aid: How We're Weaving a Safety Net, Together

The world's a bit of a rollercoaster right now, isn't it? Between the climate throwing tantrums and the economy doing its best impression of a seesaw, it feels like we're all holding on tight. But here's the thing: we don't have to do it alone. Communities everywhere are rediscovering the power of mutual aid – think of it as neighbors helping neighbors, no strings attached.

Forget Charity, this is Solidarity

Mutual aid isn't about handouts; it's about recognizing that we're all in this together. It's about saying, "Hey, I've got some extra tomatoes from my garden, want some?" or "I'm good with a hammer, let me help you fix that fence." It's about understanding that when one of us struggles, we all struggle, and when one of us thrives, we all have a chance to rise.

Real-World Heroes, Right Next Door

This isn't some abstract idea, either. Mutual aid is happening right now, all around us:

Fighting Hunger, One Fridge at a Time: "Community fridges" are popping up like wildflowers, stocked with everything from fresh veggies to leftover takeout. No judgment, just food for whoever needs it. In Detroit, the "People's Pantry" even has a van that brings groceries to folks who can't get out easily. They're not just filling bellies; they're building community.

A Roof Overhead, and a Hand Up: Housing is a mess, but tenant unions are fighting back, helping renters stand up to unfair landlords and pushing for policies that keep people in their homes. And for those who've lost their housing, mutual aid networks are stepping in with temporary shelter, warm meals, and a path towards something more stable.

Mental Health Matters: Let's face it, life can be tough on the mind. Peer support groups are creating safe spaces for people to share their struggles and find strength in numbers. And because therapy can be expensive, mutual aid funds are helping folks access the care they need without breaking the bank.

Why Mutual Aid Matters More Than Ever

Mutual aid isn't just a band-aid; it's a way to build a more resilient future. It's about recognizing our shared humanity, breaking down barriers, and creating a world where everyone has a chance to thrive. In a time of global uncertainty, mutual aid is a beacon of hope, reminding us that even when things feel chaotic, we can always count on each other.

So, What Can You Do?

Look around your neighborhood. Is there a community garden, a food pantry, or a tenant organizing group? Could you offer a skill, some time, or a bit of extra something to those in need? Every act of kindness, big or small, is a thread in the safety net we're weaving together.

Embracing Hope: How Faith Communities Light the Way Through Economic Storms

Imagine a beacon cutting through the fog of economic hardship, offering warmth and direction. That's what religious and spiritual communities do. They're more than just places of worship; they're lifelines for those struggling financially.

A Tapestry of Support

These communities wrap around those in need, offering a rich tapestry of support that goes beyond the material:

Spiritual Balm: Shared beliefs provide solace, reminding people they're not alone. Imagine a gospel choir lifting spirits with soulful hymns, or a Buddhist meditation group finding calm amidst chaos.

Guiding Lights: Religious leaders act as mentors, offering wisdom and ethical guidance. Think of a pastor counseling a family facing foreclosure, drawing strength from scripture.

Helping Hands: From food banks overflowing with donations to volunteers offering job training, faith communities become hubs of practical assistance. Picture a Sikh temple's "langar" serving hot meals to anyone who walks in, no questions asked.

Real-World Resilience

The impact is undeniable. After the 2008 financial crisis, Catholic Charities USA became a safety net for millions, providing food, housing, and job training. The Islamic Society of North America (ISNA) stepped up with health clinics and emergency aid. These are just a few examples of faith in action.

More Than Just Charity

What sets these communities apart is the emphasis on human dignity. It's not just about handouts; it's about empowerment. They help people tap into their inner strength, fostering resilience and self-reliance.

A Global Embrace

This isn't confined to any one religion or country. From bustling city churches to remote village temples, faith communities worldwide are sanctuaries in times of economic hardship. They remind us that even in the darkest of times, hope and compassion can flourish.

The Future of Support

As the world grapples with economic uncertainty, these communities will become even more vital. They're not just offering temporary relief; they're building stronger, more resilient individuals and communities. By nurturing the spirit and providing practical support, they help people weather the storm and emerge stronger on the other side.

The Threads That Bind Us: Weaving Community in a Time of Scarcity

The year is 2024, and the world feels like a ship tossed in a storm. Inflation rages, supply chains creak, and the cost of living climbs higher than ever. It's not just numbers on a screen; it's the empty space in a family's fridge, the worry lines etched on a mother's face, the simmering frustration that threatens to boil over in our communities.

As resources dwindle and competition for them intensifies, the cracks in our society widen. Old wounds of division fester, threatening to erupt into conflict. But it is precisely in these times of scarcity that we must become weavers, mending the frayed edges of our communities with threads of understanding, empathy, and shared purpose.

Community Dialogue: The Loom of Understanding

Imagine a bustling marketplace, not of goods, but of ideas. This is the power of community dialogue. It's where voices from all walks of life – the teacher, the mechanic, the entrepreneur, the student – come together to share their stories, their struggles, and their hopes.

In times of scarcity, this dialogue becomes a lifeline. It allows us to:

Unmask the Common Enemy: When we gather and speak honestly, we realize that we share the same fears and frustrations. Inflation becomes less an abstract force and more a common adversary we can face together.
Shatter the Mirrors of Misconception: Dialogue is a mirror reflecting our shared humanity. We see beyond stereotypes and labels, recognizing the anxieties and dreams that connect us.
Weave a Tapestry of Solutions: Like a vibrant tapestry, community dialogue brings together diverse threads of thought, creating innovative solutions that none of us could have imagined alone.

Empathy: The Golden Thread of Connection

Empathy is the golden thread that weaves through the fabric of a strong community. It's the ability to step into another's shoes, to feel their struggles as our own. In times of scarcity, empathy becomes a beacon of hope.

Beyond the Labels: Empathy allows us to see beyond the "haves" and "have-nots," recognizing that we are all vulnerable to life's storms.
The Ripple Effect of Kindness: A simple act of kindness, driven by empathy, can create ripples of hope that spread throughout the community. A shared meal, a listening ear, a helping hand – these are the small acts that bind us together.
Building Bridges of Trust: Empathy is the foundation of trust. When we feel understood and supported, we are more likely to reach out, to collaborate, and to build a stronger community.

Shared Goals: The Warp and Weft of a United Future

Imagine a group of weavers working together on a grand tapestry. Each person contributes their unique skills and perspectives, but they share a common vision for the final masterpiece. This is the power of shared goals.

From "Me" to "We": Shared goals transform individual struggles into collective action. We move from a mindset of scarcity to one of abundance, recognizing that we can achieve more together than we ever could alone.
Seeds of Hope: In the face of uncertainty, shared goals plant seeds of hope. They give us something to strive for, a vision of a better future that we can create together.
A Legacy of Resilience: When we work together towards shared goals, we build a more resilient community, one that can weather any storm.

Conclusion: Weaving a Tapestry of Resilience

The challenges of 2024 are a test of our collective spirit. But they are also an opportunity. An opportunity to weave a tapestry of resilience, where the threads of community dialogue, empathy, and shared goals intertwine to create a stronger, more vibrant society.

Let us embrace this opportunity. Let us become weavers of hope, mending the frayed edges of our communities and building a future where everyone belongs, everyone thrives, and everyone matters.

Investing in Ourselves: Why Community Mental Health Matters

Imagine a world where everyone has the support, they need to navigate life's challenges, to thrive even when things get tough. That's the promise of strong community mental health services. It's about more than just treating illness; it's about fostering resilience, building connections, and empowering individuals and communities to flourish.

The Reality Today

Unfortunately, we're falling short of that vision. Mental health services are often underfunded, fragmented, and shrouded in stigma. This leaves many people, especially the most vulnerable among us, struggling in silence. The pandemic has only exacerbated these challenges, casting a long shadow on our collective well-being.

The Ripple Effect of Investing in Mental Health

But there's hope. Investing in community mental health isn't just the right thing to do; it's the smart thing to do. When we prioritize mental health, we see a ripple effect of positive change:

Healthier Individuals, Stronger Communities: Access to quality care leads to better outcomes, fewer hospitalizations, and improved overall health. This translates to more vibrant, resilient communities.
Unlocking Potential: When mental health is addressed, people can return to work, school, and their passions with renewed energy and focus. This boosts productivity and strengthens our economy.
Safer Streets, More Connected Communities: Addressing mental health issues can contribute to lower crime rates and increased community safety. When people feel supported, they're less likely to fall through the cracks.
A Brighter Future for All: Effective mental health services empower individuals to live full and meaningful lives, contributing their unique talents and perspectives to society.

Building a Better System

Strengthening community mental health requires a multi-pronged approach:

Funding the Future: Governments need to step up and prioritize mental health funding. This means investing in community-based services, training programs for mental health professionals, and initiatives that promote early intervention and prevention.

Breaking Down Barriers: We need to dismantle the stigma surrounding mental illness and ensure that services are accessible to everyone, regardless of their background or circumstances. This includes providing culturally competent care, actively engaging underserved populations, and recognizing the impact of trauma on mental health.

Working Together: Collaboration is key. Integrating mental health services with primary care, schools, and other community settings can improve access and coordination of care.

Real-World Success Stories

There are inspiring examples of communities that are making a difference:

Early Psychosis Intervention Programs: These programs provide comprehensive support to young people experiencing their first episode of psychosis, helping them get back on track and achieve their full potential.

Mental Health Courts: These specialized courts divert individuals with mental illness from the criminal justice system and connect them with treatment and support services, reducing recidivism and promoting recovery.

Community-Based Crisis Response Teams: These teams provide immediate, on-site support to individuals experiencing a mental health crisis, helping de-escalate situations and connect people with the resources they need.

A Call to Action

Investing in community mental health is an investment in our collective future. It's about building a world where everyone has the opportunity to thrive, regardless of their mental health challenges. In 2024 and beyond, let's make mental health a priority. Let's build communities where everyone feels supported, valued, and empowered to live their best lives.

Chapter 9: Digital Lifeline

The Digital Couch: How Teletherapy is Reshaping Mental Healthcare
The world is changing, and so is the way we access mental health support. Forget stuffy waiting rooms and rigid schedules – teletherapy is here, and it's bringing the therapist's office straight to your screen. Imagine this: you, curled up on your couch in your pajamas, sipping tea while delving into the depths of your inner world with a qualified therapist. That's the power of online counseling.

This isn't just about convenience, though that's a huge perk. Teletherapy is a game-changer, especially for those struggling to afford traditional therapy. Let's dive into this digital revolution and explore how it's making mental wellness more accessible than ever.

Breaking Down Barriers, One Click at a Time
Teletherapy uses technology – video calls, phone sessions, even messaging – to connect you with a therapist. It's like having a mental health professional in your pocket, ready to lend an ear whenever you need it. This is a lifeline for people in remote areas, those with busy lives, or anyone who finds the traditional therapy setting intimidating.

Why Teletherapy is Making Waves:

Accessibility Unleashed: No more long drives or limited local options. With teletherapy, your location doesn't dictate your access to quality care. It's like having a world of therapists at your fingertips.
Convenience is King: Schedule sessions that fit your life, not the other way around. Early morning, late night, during your lunch break – the choice is yours.
Affordability Matters: Teletherapy often comes with a friendlier price tag. Many platforms offer sliding scale fees or subscription models, making therapy a realistic option for those on a budget.
Bye, Stigma: Seeking help can be tough. Teletherapy offers a discreet and private way to connect with a therapist, removing some of the fear and shame that can surround mental health.
Consistency is Key: Moving? Traveling? No problem. Teletherapy ensures you can maintain a consistent therapeutic relationship no matter where life takes you.

Tech-Powered Healing: Imagine journaling apps, mood trackers, and medication reminders all integrated into your therapy experience. Teletherapy platforms often offer these tools to empower you on your mental health journey.

Navigating the Digital Landscape: Challenges and Considerations
Of course, no solution is perfect. Teletherapy has its challenges:

Tech Troubles: Not everyone has reliable internet access, which can create a digital divide.
Privacy Matters: Ensuring your personal information remains confidential is crucial.
Beyond Words: While video calls help, some nuances of nonverbal communication might be lost online.
The Legal Maze: Licensing and regulations for teletherapy are still evolving, which can be confusing.
Building Connection: Establishing a strong therapeutic bond can require extra effort in a virtual setting.

Teletherapy: A Financial Lifeline
Here's where teletherapy truly shines for those facing financial constraints:

Lower Costs: Online therapy often comes at a lower cost than traditional therapy.
Travel Savings: Say goodbye to gas money and parking fees.
Pro Bono Options: Some platforms connect you with therapists offering free or reduced-fee services.
Work-Life Balance: Teletherapy's flexibility can help you avoid missing work (and losing income) for appointments.
Real Stories, Real Impact
A single mom in a rural town finds affordable therapy for her anxious teen through a teletherapy platform with sliding scale fees.
A stressed-out college student uses a subscription-based service to access unlimited messaging support during finals.
A veteran struggling with PTSD connects with a specialized therapist from the comfort of his home via teletherapy.

The Future is Virtual
Teletherapy is here to stay, and it's only getting better. Imagine virtual reality experiences and AI-powered tools enhancing therapy in ways we can only dream of. As technology advances, teletherapy will continue to evolve, breaking down barriers and making mental wellness accessible to all.

In Conclusion:

Teletherapy is revolutionizing mental healthcare, offering a lifeline to those who need it most. It's convenient, affordable, and accessible, empowering individuals to take control of their mental health journey. While challenges remain, the future of teletherapy is bright, promising a world where everyone can access the support they deserve.

The AI Revolution: Mental Health Reimagined

Forget sterile clinics and stuffy waiting rooms. The future of mental wellness is here, and it's powered by AI. Imagine a world where support is available 24/7, tailored to your unique needs, and delivered with the compassion of a therapist and the precision of an algorithm. This isn't science fiction; it's the reality we're building today.

AI Chatbots: Your Pocket-Sized Therapists

Feeling overwhelmed at 3 AM? Need to vent without judgment? AI chatbots are like having a therapist in your pocket, ready to listen and offer support whenever you need it. These digital companions use the magic of natural language processing (NLP) and machine learning (ML) to engage in genuine conversations, answer your questions, and provide evidence-based therapeutic techniques.

Woe bot: This friendly bot, developed by Stanford researchers, is like a personal CBT coach. It helps you challenge negative thoughts, manage anxiety, and develop coping mechanisms. Think of it as a digital cheerleader for your mental wellbeing!
Wyse: Need to de-stress? Wyse is your go-to for mindfulness exercises, DBT techniques, and emotional support. It's like a virtual spa day for your mind.

Tess: Tess is your personalized mental health guide, offering tailored support and integrating seamlessly with existing healthcare systems. It's like having a dedicated mental wellness concierge.

Virtual Reality Therapy: Facing Your Fears, Without the Fear

Imagine conquering your fear of public speaking by practicing in front of a virtual audience, or processing trauma in a safe, controlled environment. That's the power of VR therapy. It's like stepping into a video game designed to heal your mind.

Brave mind: Developed for veterans, Brave mind uses VR to treat PTSD by exposing users to virtual combat scenarios. It's a revolutionary way to confront trauma and reclaim your life.

Oxford VR: From anxiety disorders to phobias, Oxford VR offers immersive therapies that have shown incredible results in clinical trials. It's like rewiring your brain with the power of virtual reality.

Pisos: This platform offers a library of VR experiences for various mental health conditions, giving therapists the tools to create truly personalized treatment journeys. It's like having a virtual toolbox for mental wellness.

Beyond Chatbots and VR: The Future of Mental Healthcare

The AI revolution doesn't stop there. We're talking about:

AI-augmented diagnosis: Algorithms that analyze data from medical records, wearables, and even social media to help diagnose mental health conditions with greater accuracy and speed.

Personalized treatment recommendations: Imagine receiving treatment plans tailored to your unique needs, from therapy and medication to lifestyle changes. AI can make this a reality.

Digital biomarkers: AI can detect subtle changes in your voice, facial expressions, and even typing speed to identify early signs of mental health concerns. It's like having an early warning system for your mind.

Predictive analytics: AI can analyze data to predict the likelihood of mental health crises, allowing for proactive interventions and preventative measures. It's like having a crystal ball for your mental wellbeing.

Examples of these groundbreaking innovations include:

Ginger: This platform uses AI to personalize care and provide on-demand access to therapists and coaches. It's like having a mental health support team at your fingertips.
Mind strong: By analyzing your smartphone activity, Mind strong can assess your mental health and provide personalized interventions. It's like having a mental health tracker in your pocket.
Kintsugi: This company uses AI to analyze voice biomarkers to detect signs of depression and anxiety. It's like having a mood ring for your voice.

The Challenges and Ethical Considerations 😨

Of course, with any new technology, there are challenges to address:

Data privacy and security: Protecting sensitive mental health data is paramount.
Algorithmic bias: We must ensure AI algorithms are fair and equitable for all.
Human oversight and collaboration: AI should complement, not replace, human interaction in mental healthcare.

The Future is Bright

The intersection of AI and mental health is a beacon of hope. By harnessing the power of these technologies responsibly, we can create a world where everyone has access to the support they need, when they need it. The future of mental wellness is here, and it's powered by AI.

Bridging the Digital Gap: A Human-Centered Approach to Mental Health Access

Imagine a world where access to mental health support is as simple as opening a laptop or tapping a smartphone screen. Yet, for many, this remains a distant reality. The digital divide, like a chasm cutting through our society, separates those with access to technology from those without, disproportionately impacting marginalized communities. This isn't just about internet speed or fancy gadgets; it's about access to vital mental health resources that can change, and even save, lives.

Digital Literacy: More Than Just Clicking Buttons

Think of digital literacy as a language. If you don't speak it, a world of information remains locked away. For many in marginalized communities, navigating the online world can feel like wandering through a foreign city without a map.

Lost in Translation: Imagine an elderly woman in rural Appalachia, struggling to decipher telehealth instructions on a website. She may have spent her life relying on face-to-face interactions, and now, suddenly, she's expected to become a tech whiz.
Language Barriers: Picture a Spanish-speaking immigrant seeking online support groups, only to find a sea of English text. It's like being offered a lifeline, but in a language you don't understand.
Accessibility Overlooked: Consider a person with visual impairment trying to navigate a website with poor color contrast and tiny fonts. It's like trying to read a book in the dark.
These are not just technical issues; they are human issues. We need to go beyond simply providing internet access and focus on empowering individuals with the skills and confidence to navigate the digital landscape.

Affordability: When the Price of Connection is Too High

Access to technology shouldn't be a luxury. Yet, for many, the cost of devices, internet service, and data plans can be an insurmountable barrier.

The Weight of Financial Burden: Imagine a single mother working two jobs, struggling to put food on the table. How can she prioritize buying a laptop or paying for internet service when her family's basic needs are barely met?
Hidden Costs, Real Consequences: Even with subsidized internet, unexpected data caps can lead to overage charges, creating a financial trap for those already struggling.

We need to move beyond the simplistic notion of "connectivity" and address the complex economic realities that prevent people from accessing essential online resources.

Bridging the Gap

To truly bridge the digital divide, we need a multi-pronged approach that puts people at the center:

Investing in Infrastructure: Imagine high-speed internet reaching every corner of the country, from bustling cities to remote rural communities. This is not just about cables and wires; it's about connecting people to opportunities.
Empowering Through Digital Literacy: Imagine community centers transformed into vibrant learning hubs, where people of all ages and backgrounds can gain the skills and confidence to thrive in the digital age.
Creating Inclusive Resources: Imagine online mental health platforms available in multiple languages, designed with accessibility in mind, and culturally sensitive to the diverse needs of our communities.
This is not just about technology; it's about equity, empathy, and empowering every individual to reach their full potential. It's about building a future where access to mental health support is a right, not a privilege.

The Soul of the Machine: Navigating the Ethical Labyrinth of AI in Mental Health

Imagine a world where your deepest fears and anxieties are laid bare not to a human therapist, but to an algorithm. A world where your every digital whisper – a text message, a voice notes, a social media post – is analyzed for signs of mental distress. This is the brave new world of AI-driven mental healthcare, a realm brimming with both promise and peril.

While AI offers tantalizing solutions to the accessibility and affordability crises plaguing mental health services, we must tread carefully. Like Icarus flying too close to the sun, we risk being burned by the very technology meant to uplift us if we don't address the ethical dilemmas it presents.

The Data Dilemma: Protecting the Sacred Space of the Mind

Our minds are the last bastion of privacy, a sanctuary where our most vulnerable selves reside. Yet, AI-powered mental health tools thrive on data – the raw, unfiltered data of our inner lives. This raises profound questions:

Digital Confidentiality: Can we truly guarantee the sanctity of our mental health data in an age of rampant cyberattacks? How do we prevent our deepest fears from becoming weapons in the hands of malicious actors?
The Consent Conundrum: Are we truly informed when we click "agree" on those lengthy terms and conditions? Do we understand the implications of our data being shared, analyzed, and potentially commercialized?
Who Owns Your Mind? In this digital age, do we still retain ownership of our thoughts and feelings, or do they become commodities in the data marketplace?
Think of a mental health app that tracks your mood based on your social media activity. While seemingly innocuous, this app could inadvertently reveal deeply personal information to developers or even advertisers. The Cambridge Analytica scandal serves as a chilling reminder of how personal data can be exploited for political manipulation. Do we want our mental health data to suffer the same fate?

The Algorithmic Bias Blindspot: When AI Perpetuates Prejudice

AI algorithms are not objective oracles; they are products of their creators and the data they are trained on. This can lead to algorithmic bias, where the very tools meant to help us end up reinforcing existing societal prejudices.

The Data Distortion: If an algorithm is trained primarily on data from privileged populations, it may fail to recognize or misinterpret the mental health struggles of marginalized communities.
The Design Flaw: Even the design of an algorithm can embed bias. Imagine an AI-powered therapy tool that relies on facial expression analysis. If this tool is trained on predominantly white faces, it may

misinterpret the expressions of people of color, leading to misdiagnosis and inappropriate treatment.

Consider the real-world example of risk assessment algorithms used in the US criminal justice system. These algorithms have been shown to be biased against Black defendants, predicting higher recidivism rates even when controlling for other factors. This algorithmic prejudice can perpetuate systemic racism and deny individuals fair treatment.

The Human-Technology Tightrope: Balancing Innovation with Empathy

Perhaps the most profound ethical question is how AI will impact the human-technology relationship in mental healthcare.

The Therapist-Patient Bond: Can a machine truly replicate the empathy, understanding, and human connection that form the bedrock of the therapeutic alliance?

The AI Overseer: While AI can assist with diagnosis and treatment, should it ever be allowed to make decisions autonomously? How do we ensure human oversight and prevent the dehumanization of care?

Bridging the Digital Divide: Will AI democratize access to mental healthcare, or will it exacerbate existing inequalities? How do we ensure these technologies are accessible and culturally sensitive for all?

Think of Woe bot, the AI-powered chatbot therapist. While Woe bot can provide valuable support and coping strategies, it can never replace the nuanced understanding and empathy of a human therapist. Similarly, virtual reality exposure therapy, while promising, cannot replicate the safety and support of a real-world therapeutic setting.

Charting a Responsible Course: A Call to Action

The ethical challenges posed by AI in mental health demand a collective response. We need:

Ethical Guardrails: Clear guidelines and regulations are needed to protect data privacy, address algorithmic bias, and ensure human oversight.

Transparency and Explain ability: AI algorithms should be transparent and explainable, so users understand how decisions are being made about their mental health.

Diversity and Inclusion: AI development must prioritize diversity and inclusion, ensuring these technologies are accessible and effective for all populations.

The Human-Centered Approach: We must never lose sight of the human element in mental healthcare. AI should be a tool to augment, not replace, the human connection.

The journey into the world of AI-driven mental healthcare is fraught with ethical complexities. By embracing a human-centered approach, prioritizing ethical considerations, and fostering open dialogue, we can harness the power of AI to create a more just and compassionate mental healthcare system for all.

Chapter 10: Inflation and Social Unrest

The Price We Pay: When Inflation Fuels the Fires of Discontent

Imagine a world where the cost of living is a relentless uphill climb, where your paycheck feels lighter with each passing month, and the things you once took for granted become luxuries. This is the reality for millions grappling with the corrosive effects of inflation, a silent thief that erodes purchasing power and fuels a burning sense of injustice known as relative deprivation.

More Than Just Empty Pockets

Relative deprivation isn't simply about lacking material wealth; it's the gnawing feeling that you're falling behind while others prosper. It's the sting of comparison, the frustration of seeing your dreams slip further out of reach as prices soar. This sense of unfairness can fester and grow, transforming into resentment and simmering social unrest.

Inflation: The Catalyst of Discontent

Inflation acts like a magnifying glass, amplifying existing inequalities and creating new fault lines in society. As prices climb, those at the bottom rungs of the economic ladder are hit hardest. Their incomes, already stretched thin, are further strained, leaving them with impossible choices between basic necessities.

This economic squeeze fosters a sense of powerlessness and vulnerability. People watch their hard-earned money evaporate, their hopes for a better future dimming with each passing day. Trust in institutions crumbles as the gap between the haves and have-nots widens.

The Psychological Scars of Rising Prices

The impact of inflation extends far beyond the financial realm. It seeps into our minds, breeding anxiety, stress, and a profound sense of insecurity. The constant struggle to make ends meet takes a toll on mental well-being, leaving individuals feeling trapped and hopeless.

From Whispers to Uprising: The Seeds of Social Unrest

History whispers a cautionary tale. Time and again, economic hardship and perceived injustice have ignited the flames of social unrest. From the French Revolution to the Arab Spring, the echoes of discontent reverberate through the ages.

The Yellow Vest movement in France, the 2022 Sri Lankan protests, and the 2023 Pakistan economic crisis stand as stark reminders of the power of relative deprivation to mobilize masses. These movements, born out of frustration and a yearning for change, underscore the urgent need to address the root causes of economic inequality.

A Path Forward: Healing the Wounds of Inequality

Mitigating the impact of relative deprivation demands a multi-pronged approach. Governments must implement policies that promote economic growth, reduce inequality, and ensure that the fruits of prosperity are shared equitably. Progressive taxation, social safety nets, and investments in education and healthcare are crucial steps in the right direction.

But economic measures alone are not enough. We must also address the psychological scars of inflation and foster a sense of social cohesion. Public education campaigns can help raise awareness about the causes and consequences of inflation, while counseling and support services can provide a lifeline to those struggling with economic hardship.

A Shared Responsibility

Creating a more just and equitable society requires a collective effort. We must bridge the divides that separate us, promote dialogue and understanding, and work together to build a world where everyone has the opportunity to thrive. Only then can we extinguish the fires of discontent and ensure that the price of progress is not paid by the most vulnerable among us.

The Boiling Point: When Economic Hardship Turns Up the Heat

Imagine a pot simmering on the stove. Inside, the ingredients of daily life bubble away: work, family, hopes, and dreams. But what happens when the heat gets cranked up? When bills pile high, jobs disappear, and the gap between the haves and have-nots yawns wider? The pot boils over. That's the frustration-aggression hypothesis in action.

The Pressure Cooker Within

Economic hardship isn't just about empty wallets; it's about the pressure cooker of stress it creates inside our minds. When we can't provide for ourselves or our loved ones, when dreams feel out of reach, frustration simmers. It can morph into anger – a volatile fuel that can ignite aggressive actions.

Think of it like this:

Blocked Goals: We all have goals, big and small. Economic hardship throws up roadblocks, leaving us feeling stuck and powerless.
Stress Overload: Financial worries are a heavy burden. They chip away at our coping mechanisms, leaving us vulnerable to lashing out.
The Comparison Game: In a world of Instagram influencers and "Keeping Up with the Joneses," it's easy to feel like we're falling behind. This sense of relative deprivation adds fuel to the fire.
Learned Helplessness: When struggles seem endless, we can fall into a trap of learned helplessness. We feel like nothing we do matters, and that hopelessness can breed anger.

From Personal Pain to Social Explosion

This pressure cooker effect doesn't just impact individuals; it can boil over into society as a whole. When large groups of people experience economic hardship, it creates a shared sense of frustration and injustice. Think of it as a collective pressure cooker:

Strength in Numbers: Shared hardship can forge strong bonds between people. This can be a force for positive change, but it can also lead to social unrest and even violence if frustrations aren't addressed.

Finding a Scapegoat: In tough times, it's easy to look for someone to blame. This can lead to prejudice and discrimination against groups perceived as "different" or "better off."
The Revolution Spark: History is filled with examples of economic hardship fueling revolutions and uprisings. The French Revolution, the Arab Spring – these were moments when collective frustration reached a boiling point.

Cooling the Flames

Understanding the link between economic hardship and aggression is key to finding solutions. We need to address the root causes of inequality, provide support for those struggling, and teach healthy ways to cope with frustration. Here are some ideas:

Safety Nets: Strong social programs act as a safety net, preventing people from falling into despair when hardship strikes.
Opportunity Knocks: Access to education, job training, and affordable housing can help people build a better future and break the cycle of poverty.
Conflict Resolution: Teaching people how to handle conflict constructively can prevent frustration from escalating into aggression.
A Spark of Hope

Economic hardship can create a breeding ground for anger and violence, but it's not inevitable. By understanding the psychological forces at play, we can work towards a society where everyone has the opportunity to thrive. Even in the face of hardship, we must nurture hope, resilience, and a belief in our ability to create a better future.

The Inflation Fault Line: How Rising Prices Crack Society

Imagine a wildfire. Inflation is the heat, drying out the underbrush of our social fabric. Suddenly, the smallest spark – a political jab, a misplaced fear – ignites a blaze of division. It's not just about empty wallets; it's about who we blame when the flames start licking at our heels.

The 'Us vs. Them' of Empty Pockets

When prices soar, we feel vulnerable, like the ground is shifting beneath our feet. Our instinct? Cling tighter to 'our people' – those who share our background, beliefs, or struggles. It's classic 'Social Identity Theory' in action: when times get tough, our group identity becomes a life raft in a sea of uncertainty.

But this life raft has a dark side. As we pull closer to 'us,' we push away 'them' – the 'others' who become scapegoats for our economic anxieties. Suddenly, immigrants are stealing jobs, the wealthy are hoarding resources, and the government is the enemy. This isn't just a rational response to hardship; it's an emotional survival mechanism, and it can be dangerously manipulated.

Fanning the Flames of Fear

Politicians and pundits know this. They become arsonists, tossing inflammatory rhetoric onto the fire. They paint vivid pictures of 'outsiders' as the cause of our suffering, fueling resentment and turning neighbors against each other. History is littered with examples – the Nazis blaming Jews for Germany's economic woes, populist movements demonizing immigrants after the 2008 financial crisis.

Building Firebreaks: How to Stop the Blaze

So, how do we douse these flames before they consume us?

Economic First Aid: Address the root causes of hardship. Fair wages, affordable housing, and strong social safety nets act like fire retardant, making our communities less susceptible to the flames of division.
Shared Prosperity: Ensure everyone benefits from economic growth. A rising tide should lift all boats, not just the yachts.
Calling Out the Arsonists: Challenge divisive rhetoric. Don't let fearmongers exploit our anxieties for their own gain.
Bridging the Divide: Encourage dialogue and understanding between different groups. Shared meals, community projects, and honest conversations can help us see each other as humans, not just 'us' and 'them.'

Inflation might be an economic problem, but its consequences are deeply social. By understanding the psychology of division, we can build a society that's resilient to the flames of fear and prejudice. It's time to stop throwing gasoline on the fire and start working together to extinguish it.

Subtopic 4: Weaving Peace Together: How Communities Can Rise Above and Find Strength in the Face of Conflict

Introduction

Imagine a world where every community hums with the quiet rhythm of peace, where differences are celebrated, and where the wounds of conflict heal into powerful scars of resilience. This is the world we yearn for, and while the path to peace can be winding and challenging, it's a journey we must embark on together. In this exploration, we'll delve into the heart of building community resilience and addressing the economic injustices that often fan the flames of unrest. We'll discover how dialogue, empathy, and social justice initiatives can be the threads that weave together the fabric of a peaceful and harmonious society.

Unraveling the Roots of Social Unrest

Social unrest, like a storm, arises from a complex convergence of factors. Economic disparities, where poverty and inequality cast long shadows, often act as the tempestuous winds that fuel discontent. When people feel trapped in a cycle of economic hardship, a sense of frustration and powerlessness can take root, eventually erupting into social unrest.

Discrimination, lack of political representation, and the violation of human rights are like lightning strikes that ignite tensions further. When voices are silenced and rights are trampled upon, people may feel compelled to take collective action to demand change and justice.

Building Unbreakable Communities

Imagine a community as a sturdy tree, its roots deeply intertwined, capable of weathering the fiercest storms. This is the essence of community resilience - the ability to not only withstand adversity but to emerge stronger from it. A resilient community is like a well-tended garden, where the seeds of peace are nurtured and allowed to blossom.

Here are some key strategies to cultivate community resilience:

Strengthening Social Bonds: Just as a tapestry is made strong by the interwoven threads, a community's resilience lies in the strength of its social connections. When neighbors know and support each other, they are less likely to resort to violence or destructive behavior.

Promoting Inclusive Governance: A community where everyone has a voice is like a well-tuned orchestra, where each instrument contributes to a harmonious melody. Inclusive governance ensures that all members of the community participate in decision-making, addressing grievances before they escalate into conflict.

Empowering Marginalized Groups: Imagine a society where everyone has the opportunity to shine, regardless of their background. Empowering marginalized groups, providing them with education, resources, and opportunities, is crucial for creating a just and equitable society.

Building Trust in Institutions: Trust in institutions is like the foundation of a house; without it, the structure is unstable. When people believe that institutions are fair and impartial, they are more likely to abide by the law and resolve disputes peacefully.

The Power of Dialogue, Empathy, and Social Justice

Dialogue, empathy, and social justice are the guiding stars that illuminate the path to peace.

Dialogue: Imagine a world where people truly listen to each other, seeking understanding rather than conflict. Open and inclusive dialogue can bridge divides, build empathy, and address grievances before they escalate into violence.

Empathy: Empathy is like a bridge that connects people, allowing them to see the world through each other's eyes. Cultivating empathy can help break down stereotypes and prejudices, fostering compassion and understanding.

Social Justice Initiatives: Addressing the root causes of social unrest, such as poverty, inequality, and discrimination, is like tending to the soil of a garden, ensuring that the seeds of peace have fertile ground to grow. Social justice initiatives create a more just and equitable society, reducing the likelihood of conflict.

Stories of Hope and Healing

Let's explore some inspiring examples of communities that have successfully navigated the path to peace:

Rwanda: After the devastating genocide in 1994, Rwanda has made remarkable strides in promoting peace and reconciliation. Through community-based justice mechanisms, national unity programs, and economic development initiatives, Rwanda has shown the world the power of healing and forgiveness.

Northern Ireland: The Good Friday Agreement of 1998 marked a turning point in the decades-long conflict in Northern Ireland. By establishing power-sharing institutions, recognizing the rights of both communities, and addressing economic and social inequalities, Northern Ireland has demonstrated the power of dialogue and compromise.

South Africa: The Truth and Reconciliation Commission (TRC), established after the end of apartheid, played a crucial role in healing the wounds of the past. By providing a platform for victims and perpetrators to share their stories, acknowledge past injustices, and seek forgiveness, South Africa has shown the world the transformative power of truth and reconciliation.

Conclusion

Building peace is like weaving a tapestry, where each thread represents a crucial element: dialogue, empathy, social justice, and community resilience. By embracing these elements, we can create a world where peace is not just an aspiration but a living reality. Let us all be weavers of peace, contributing our unique threads to the rich tapestry of humanity.

Chapter 11: Trust in Crisis

The Psychology of Trust: Why Inflation Can Undermine Confidence in Government and Economic Systems

Introduction

Imagine trust as the invisible glue that holds our society and economy together. It's the feeling of reliability and confidence we have in our institutions, our economic systems, and even our currency. But when inflation rears its ugly head, this glue starts to melt away, leaving behind uncertainty, insecurity, and even resentment towards those in power.

Factors that Contribute to Trust in Institutions

Trust in institutions, whether governmental or economic, is a delicate flower that blooms from a combination of factors:

Performance and competence: Institutions need to prove their worth by effectively fulfilling their duties. A government consistently failing to provide basic services or an economic system riddled with instability will inevitably lose the public's trust.
Transparency and accountability: Open communication and clear lines of responsibility are essential. People need to understand how decisions are made and who is accountable for them. A lack of transparency breeds suspicion and erodes trust.
Fairness and equity: Institutions must be perceived as just and impartial. If people believe the system is rigged in favor of certain groups or that their voices are not heard, trust will dwindle.
Stability and predictability: A sense of stability and predictability is crucial for trust. People need to believe that the rules of the game won't change arbitrarily and that their institutions can weather economic storms.
Leadership and vision: Strong, ethical leadership that inspires confidence and articulates a clear vision for the future is vital for building and maintaining trust.

How Inflation Disrupts These Factors

Inflation acts like a destructive pest, nibbling away at these trust-building factors:

Reduced performance and competence: Inflation erodes the purchasing power of individuals and businesses, making it harder to make ends meet and plan for the future. This can lead to a perception that the government and economic institutions are failing to manage the economy effectively.
Loss of transparency and accountability: Inflation can be a complex phenomenon with multiple causes, making it difficult for the average person to understand what is happening and who is responsible. This lack of clarity can create a sense that those in power are either incompetent or deliberately hiding information.
Increased inequality: Inflation often disproportionately affects those with lower incomes, who have fewer assets to protect against rising prices. This can exacerbate existing inequalities and lead to a sense of unfairness and resentment.
Heightened uncertainty and instability: Inflation creates uncertainty about the future, making it difficult for individuals and businesses to plan and invest. This instability can further erode trust in the economic system.
Diminished leadership and vision: In times of high inflation, leaders may struggle to articulate a clear path forward, leading to a perception of weakness and lack of direction.

Examples and Case Studies

History is littered with examples of how inflation has undermined trust in institutions and led to social and political unrest:

Weimar Republic (Germany, 1920s): Hyperinflation in post-World War I Germany destroyed the value of the currency, wiping out savings and causing widespread economic chaos. This led to a deep distrust of the government and paved the way for the rise of extremist ideologies.
Latin America (1970s and 1980s): Many Latin American countries experienced high inflation during this period, leading to social unrest, political instability, and a decline in trust in democratic institutions.

Zimbabwe (2000s): Hyperinflation in Zimbabwe reached astronomical levels, rendering the currency virtually worthless and causing widespread poverty and suffering. This led to a complete breakdown of trust in the government and the economic system.
Venezuela (2010s): Hyperinflation in Venezuela, coupled with political repression and economic mismanagement, has led to a humanitarian crisis, mass emigration, and a deep distrust of the government.

The Psychological Impact of Inflation

Beyond its economic consequences, inflation also has a profound psychological impact on individuals and society:

Loss of control: Inflation can make people feel like they are losing control of their lives and finances. This can lead to anxiety, stress, and a sense of helplessness.
Erosion of social cohesion: Inflation can create divisions within society, as people compete for scarce resources and blame each other for their economic woes.
Decline in morale: A prolonged period of high inflation can lead to a general decline in morale and a loss of faith in the future.
Increased risk aversion: Inflation can make people more risk-averse, leading to a decline in investment and economic growth.

Conclusion

Inflation is not just an economic problem; it's a social and psychological one. By eroding trust in institutions, creating uncertainty, and fueling social divisions, inflation can undermine the very foundations of a healthy society and economy. Therefore, it's crucial for governments and central banks to maintain price stability and communicate clearly and transparently with the public about the challenges and solutions to inflation. Only then can trust be restored and the economy put back on a path to sustainable growth.

The Blame Game: How Inflation Can Tear Us Apart

Imagine a fire slowly spreading through a house. That's what inflation is like. It starts small, maybe you notice the price of milk creeping up, or your favorite restaurant's menu suddenly seems a bit pricier. But as it spreads, this "fire" starts to consume everything – your savings, your peace of mind, and even the bonds that hold our society together.

Inflation isn't just about numbers; it's about fear and frustration. It's about that gnawing feeling in your gut when you realize your paycheck doesn't stretch as far as it used to. And when people are scared and frustrated, they look for someone to blame.

Suddenly, everyone's pointing fingers. Politicians thunder about the other party's reckless spending, while talk radio hosts rant about greedy corporations and "outsiders" stealing our jobs. Social media becomes a battleground of accusations and insults, as people vent their anxieties on anyone who seems different or holds opposing views.

This blame game is incredibly dangerous. It's like throwing gasoline on that fire, making it burn even hotter and faster. It divides us into warring tribes, each convinced that the other is the enemy. Trust erodes, friendships fracture, and community's crumble.

History is full of examples where inflation's flames have fanned the embers of hatred and division. In Weimar Germany, hyperinflation created the perfect breeding ground for the Nazis' poisonous ideology. In the 1970s, America's "stagflation" fueled social unrest and political polarization. And today, in Venezuela, economic chaos has pushed a once-vibrant nation to the brink of collapse.

But there's hope. We can fight this fire, not with more blame and division, but with understanding and cooperation. We need leaders who will tell the truth about inflation's complex causes, instead of exploiting it for political gain. We need to invest in education and social programs that lift people out of poverty and reduce inequality. And most importantly, we need to rediscover our shared humanity, remembering that we're all in this together.

Inflation may be a formidable foe, but it's not unbeatable. By working together, with empathy and compassion, we can extinguish its flames and rebuild a stronger, more united society.

Restoring Trust in Uncertain Times: A Beacon of Hope

Imagine a ship navigating a storm. The waves crash, the winds howl, and fear grips the hearts of those onboard. But amidst the chaos, a beacon of light shines – the unwavering trust in the captain and crew.

Economic uncertainty can feel like a storm, tossing and turning our lives. Anxiety and distrust loom large. Yet, like that ship, we can weather the storm if we have trust in our leaders and institutions.

Transparency: Shining a Light in the Darkness

Transparency is the lighthouse that guides us through the storm. It means being open and honest, like a captain who keeps the passengers informed about the challenges ahead. Governments and institutions must act like that captain, sharing clear and accurate information about the economic situation. They need to explain the course they're charting and the reasons behind their decisions.

Think of it as a map that everyone can access. In today's digital age, this map should be online, with real-time updates on the economic climate. Just as a ship's navigator uses charts and instruments, we need readily available data and user-friendly platforms to understand the economic landscape.

Accountability: Steering the Ship with Responsibility

Accountability is the rudder that keeps the ship on course. It's about taking responsibility for decisions and being held answerable for the outcomes. Leaders must act like the first mate, ensuring that the ship is steered in the right direction and that resources are used wisely.

Clear lines of responsibility are like the different roles on a ship – everyone knows their duty. Independent oversight bodies act as the coastguard, keeping a watchful eye on the ship's journey and ensuring it stays on the right path. And when mistakes happen, it's like the captain acknowledging a navigational error and taking corrective action.

Effective Communication: Calming the Storm with Words

Effective communication is the calming voice of the captain that reassures the passengers. It's about conveying information with empathy and clarity, like a soothing message broadcast over the ship's intercom. Leaders need to understand the fears and anxieties people face during economic hardship and offer support and reassurance.

Imagine the captain tailoring their communication to different groups on the ship – the crew, the passengers, and those who might need extra assistance. This is what our leaders must do, crafting messages that resonate with various segments of the population.

Case Studies: Lessons from Past Voyages

The 2008 financial crisis was like a massive storm that nearly capsized the global economy. In its aftermath, many countries took steps to improve transparency and accountability in the financial sector, like reinforcing the ship's hull to withstand future storms.

The COVID-19 pandemic was another unexpected tempest. Countries that communicated clearly and transparently, like New Zealand and South Korea, were like ships that navigated the storm more effectively, keeping their passengers safe and informed.

Conclusion: Reaching Safe Harbor Together

Restoring trust during economic uncertainty is like guiding a ship through a storm and safely reaching the harbor. Transparency, accountability, and effective communication are the compass, rudder, and captain's voice that will lead us through these turbulent waters. Trust is the anchor that keeps us steady, and it's something that must be earned and nurtured. By working together, we can weather any economic storm and emerge stronger on the other side.

The Media's Balancing Act: Walking the Tightrope Between Information and Panic in Economic Storms

Imagine the economy as a tightrope walker gracefully balancing in the wind. The media acts as the safety net below, but a poorly positioned net can do more harm than good. In times of economic turbulence, like the inflationary headwinds we face today, the media's role becomes even more critical. It's a delicate dance between informing the public and inadvertently fueling the flames of panic.

The Echo Chamber of Fear: How Media Narratives Shape Our Economic Reality

Think of the media as a powerful amplifier. When it focuses solely on rising prices, empty shelves, and struggling businesses, it amplifies our anxieties. This 'doom and gloom' narrative can become a self-fulfilling prophecy. Consumers, gripped by fear, tighten their purse strings, businesses hesitate to invest, and the economy spirals further downward.

However, the media can also be a beacon of hope. By providing context, explaining the 'why' behind the 'what', and highlighting stories of resilience, it can foster a sense of calm and collective determination.

The Ethical Compass: Navigating the Treacherous Waters of Economic Reporting

In the stormy seas of economic crises, ethical journalism is the compass guiding us towards safe harbor. It demands:

Truth as the Anchor: Fact-checking becomes paramount. Every statistic, every expert quote, must be rigorously vetted.
Sensationalism Overboard: Catchy headlines and dramatic visuals should never come at the expense of accuracy.
Context is King: Economic data without context is like a ship without a rudder. Journalists must explain the intricate web of cause and effect.
A Chorus of Voices: The narrative shouldn't be dominated by a single perspective. Give voice to economists, business owners, and everyday people grappling with the crisis.

Learning from the Past: Echoes of Economic Crises in the Media Mirror

History is littered with examples of how media narratives shaped economic events:

The Great Depression: A relentless focus on hardship deepened the sense of despair, prolonging the crisis.
The 2008 Financial Crisis: While some outlets delved into the complexities, others focused on the drama, eroding trust in the system.
The COVID-19 Pandemic: A mix of vital information and fear-mongering created a volatile information landscape.

Charting a Course for Responsible Reporting

To ensure the media acts as a stabilizing force, we need:

Investing in Navigators: Journalists need specialized training to decode economic jargon and translate it for the public.
Embracing Nuance: Economic crises are rarely black and white. The media must embrace complexity and avoid simplistic narratives.
Ethical Guardrails: News organizations need clear guidelines on fact-checking, sourcing, and avoiding conflicts of interest.
Empowering the Audience: We, the audience, must become critical consumers of information, seeking diverse sources and challenging biases.

The Bottom Line:

In the high-stakes drama of economic crises, the media wields immense power. By embracing ethical reporting, prioritizing context, and avoiding sensationalism, it can help us weather the storm and emerge stronger on the other side.

Chapter 12: Political Polarization

The Politics of Panic: How Economic Anxieties Pull Our Strings

Imagine your brain as a car. Logic and reason are usually at the wheel, carefully navigating the roads of decision-making. But when fear and anxiety creep in, they slam on the gas, hijacking the controls and sending you careening down a path you might not otherwise choose.

This is especially true when the economy throws a curveball. Job insecurity, rising prices, and a general sense of "things falling apart" can transform us into jittery passengers, desperate for someone to grab the wheel and steer us to safety.

Politicians know this all too well. They become psychological mechanics, exploiting our anxieties and offering quick fixes, often in the form of scapegoats and simplistic solutions. It's like they're selling us a shiny new car with the promise of a smooth ride, even if it's headed straight for a cliff.

The Fear Factor: A Deep Dive into Our Anxious Minds

Our brains are wired to prioritize survival. Fear is that primal alarm bell, warning us of danger and triggering the urge to fight or flee. Anxiety is its more subtle cousin, a nagging worry about what might happen.

In uncertain times, these emotions become supercharged. We crave certainty, and politicians offer it in the form of strong leadership, bold promises, and a comforting sense of "us vs. them." It's a seductive cocktail, especially when served with a side of fear-mongering.

The Anxiety Election: Case Studies in Fear-Driven Politics

Think back to the 2008 financial crisis. The world felt like it was teetering on the brink, and populist movements surged, offering simple solutions and blaming "outsiders" for our troubles. It was a classic case of fear and anxiety driving voters into the arms of those who promised to restore order, even at the cost of reason and compassion.

The Brexit vote was another prime example. Fear of immigration, economic decline, and loss of control fueled a campaign that traded on anxieties, ultimately leading to a decision that continues to reverberate today.

And who could forget the 2020 US Presidential Election? A global pandemic, social unrest, and a deeply divided nation created the perfect storm of anxiety. Both candidates tapped into our fears, painting a bleak picture of the future if the "other side" won.

Taming the Beast: How to Navigate the Politics of Panic

So, how do we avoid becoming puppets in the theater of fear? Here are a few ideas:

Become an Emotion Detective: Learn to recognize when fear and anxiety are clouding your judgment. Ask yourself: "Is this decision based on facts and logic, or am I being swayed by emotions?"
Challenge the Narrative: Don't blindly accept the fear-mongering narratives peddled by politicians and the media. Seek out diverse perspectives, fact-check information, and engage in critical thinking.
Embrace Emotional Intelligence: Cultivate self-awareness and empathy. Understand your own emotional triggers and recognize how others might be feeling. This will help you navigate political discourse with more compassion and less reactivity.
Remember, fear and anxiety are natural human emotions, but they shouldn't be the sole drivers of our political choices. By cultivating awareness, critical thinking, and emotional intelligence, we can reclaim control of the wheel and steer ourselves towards a more informed and compassionate future.

The "Us vs. Them" Mentality: When Inflation Fans the Flames of Fear

Imagine Maria, a single mother in a bustling city. As prices climb, her weekly grocery trip becomes a tightrope walk between necessities and empty shelves. The gnawing sense of lack, that primal fear of not having enough, creeps in. She sees the news, filled with stories of economic turmoil, of "others" getting ahead while she falls behind. Resentment simmers. It's a feeling echoed in hushed conversations at the school gate, in frustrated online rants, in the growing chasm between "us" and "them."

Inflation, that silent thief, doesn't just steal our purchasing power; it steals our sense of security, our trust in the system, and sometimes, our compassion for each other. It's like a disease, spreading through the veins of society, turning neighbor against neighbor.

Remember the Weimar Republic, where hyperinflation fueled the rise of Nazism? Picture those desperate times: families burning worthless banknotes for warmth, fear turning to hate as scapegoats were sought. Or consider Rwanda, where economic hardship fanned the flames of ethnic tensions, culminating in unspeakable horrors.

These aren't just historical footnotes. The world is facing a new wave of inflation, and the echoes of the past ring alarmingly loud. Political polarization deepens, fueled by social media echo chambers and fear-mongering politicians. Social unrest bubbles over, with protests erupting in cities across the globe.

But amidst the darkness, sparks of humanity flicker. A community garden blooms in a struggling neighborhood, bringing together families from all walks of life. A food bank volunteer shares a warm meal and a kind word with someone who has lost everything. These acts of resistance, of choosing empathy over fear, remind us that we are not just victims of circumstance.

We have a choice. We can succumb to the "us vs. them" mentality, building walls and pointing fingers. Or we can choose to understand, to bridge divides, to build a world where everyone feels safe and valued.

This isn't just about economics; it's about our shared humanity. It's about recognizing that we're all in this sinking boat together, and the only way to survive is to bail water together.

What can you do?

Challenge your own biases. When you feel that "us vs. them" instinct kicking in, take a step back. Question your assumptions. Seek out diverse perspectives.
Connect with your community. Join local initiatives that promote inclusivity and support those in need.
Amplify voices of compassion. Share stories of hope and resilience. Challenge divisive narratives online and offline.
The fight against inflation isn't just about numbers; it's about reclaiming our shared humanity. Let's choose empathy over fear, and build a world where everyone has a place at the table.

The Echo Chamber's Embrace: How Social Media Fuels the Fires of Political Polarization

In our hyper-connected world, social media has become the town square of the 21st century, the place where we gather to debate, discuss, and dissect the issues of the day. Yet, for all its promise of open dialogue and connection, social media also harbors a darker side, one where echo chambers and filter bubbles thrive, amplifying political polarization to a fever pitch.

Imagine a world where every voice you hear echoes your own beliefs, where every article you read confirms your existing biases. This is the reality of the echo chamber, a digital cocoon where dissenting opinions are silenced and critical thinking is stifled. Social media, with its sophisticated algorithms and personalized feeds, has become the architect of these echo chambers, curating our online experiences to show us only what we want to see.

But the danger goes beyond mere isolation. In these echo chambers, misinformation spreads like wildfire, its flames fanned by the winds of confirmation bias. Conspiracy theories take root, and partisan divides deepen, leaving us trapped in a self-perpetuating cycle of distrust and animosity.

The consequences are all too real. We've seen how echo chambers can fuel political extremism, leading to real-world violence and social unrest. We've witnessed how filter bubbles can distort our understanding of the world, leaving us vulnerable to manipulation and propaganda.

So how do we break free from these digital prisons? It starts with recognizing the power of algorithms and the biases they perpetuate. We must become more discerning consumers of information, seeking out diverse perspectives and challenging our own assumptions.

Social media platforms also have a role to play. They must take responsibility for the algorithms they create and the echo chambers they foster. By promoting transparency and giving users more control over their feeds, they can help create a more balanced and inclusive online environment.

Ultimately, the fight against political polarization is a fight for our collective sanity. It's a fight to reclaim the promise of social media as a tool for connection and understanding. By breaking down the walls of echo chambers and embracing the diversity of thought, we can build a more informed, more tolerant, and more united society.

"We're Living in Echo Chambers – How Do We Break Free?"

You ever feel like you're stuck in a bubble? Like everyone around you just agrees with everything you say, and anyone who doesn't is basically the enemy? Yeah, that's our world now. We've got our "red" corners and our "blue" corners, and nobody dares cross the line.

It's like what happened to my friend Sarah. She's a die-hard liberal, and she was always posting these fiery political rants on Facebook. One day, she got into this huge argument with her uncle, who's super conservative. They were both saying really hurtful things, and it ended with them unfriending each other. It actually tore the whole family apart for a while.

It's not just politics, either. It's everything! The music we listen to, the food we eat, even the way we raise our kids. We're so busy shouting our opinions from the rooftops that we forget to actually listen to each other.

But here's the thing: deep down, we all want the same things, right? We want a good life for ourselves and our families. We want a safe community. We want a future where our kids can thrive.

So, how do we get past all this noise and find that common ground?

Maybe we start by actually talking to each other. Not arguing, not debating, but listening. Really trying to understand where the other person is coming from. Like that time our town had that huge debate about the new park. People were at each other's throats! But then, they organized these community meetings where folks could just share their concerns and ideas. You know what? They actually found a solution that worked for everyone!

Maybe we look for the things we have in common, even if it's just a love for our town's terrible football team or a shared addiction to spicy tacos. I remember this one Thanksgiving dinner – my family's pretty mixed politically. Things were getting tense, and then my grandma starts talking about her prize-winning pumpkin pie recipe. Suddenly, everyone's laughing and sharing stories about their baking disasters. It totally shifted the mood!

Maybe we admit that we don't have all the answers. That sometimes, the other side might actually have a point. I used to think anyone who drove a big truck was just a gas-guzzling polluter. Then I met this guy, a farmer, who explained how he needs his truck for his work, and how he's actually doing a ton to conserve water and protect the soil. It totally changed my perspective.

I know it sounds cheesy, but I really believe we can do better. We can disagree without hating each other. We can find solutions together, even if we don't see eye-to-eye on everything.

It starts with each of us. It starts with a willingness to listen, to understand, and to find that little spark of connection that reminds us we're all human.

Chapter 13: Rethinking Economic Policy

Beyond GDP: Is it Time to Reimagine How We Measure Progress?

Imagine a world where economic success isn't just about cold, hard cash. A world where the well-being of people, the health of our planet, and the strength of our communities share the spotlight with traditional economic measures. This isn't a utopian dream, but a growing movement gaining traction worldwide.

For decades, Gross Domestic Product (GDP) has been the undisputed king of economic indicators, the yardstick by which we measure a nation's progress. But like a faded monarch clinging to power, GDP is increasingly being challenged. Why? Because it simply doesn't tell the whole story.

Think of it like this: GDP is like judging a restaurant solely on its revenue. A packed house might seem impressive, but what if the food is terrible, the staff miserable, and the kitchen a health hazard? Similarly, a country with a booming GDP might be hiding deep social inequalities, environmental destruction, or a population struggling with mental health issues.

The Cracks in the Crown: Why GDP Falls Short

GDP, in its relentless pursuit of measuring market activity, overlooks some critical aspects of what truly makes a society thrive:

The Unseen Workhorses: It ignores the invaluable contributions of unpaid labor – the stay-at-home parents, the community volunteers, the caregivers who keep our society functioning.
The Price of Progress: GDP often fails to account for the environmental cost of economic growth, treating pollution and resource depletion as mere byproducts of "progress."
The Inequality Puzzle: A rising GDP can mask widening gaps between the rich and the poor, leaving a significant portion of society behind.
The Human Factor: GDP is blind to the social and psychological well-being of citizens. A nation can be wealthy on paper yet suffer from high levels of stress, loneliness, and mental health problems.

A New Era: Embracing Well-being Metrics

The good news is that a paradigm shift is underway. Policymakers, researchers, and even some governments are starting to look beyond GDP and embrace a more holistic approach to measuring progress. This means considering factors like:

Mental and physical health: How happy and healthy are citizens?
Social connections: How strong are community bonds?
Environmental sustainability: Are we preserving our planet for future generations?
Education and skills: Are people equipped to thrive in the modern world?
Work-life balance: Are people able to enjoy fulfilling lives outside of work?
Income equality: Is wealth distributed fairly?

Pioneers of Progress: Real-World Examples

The shift towards well-being is more than just a lofty ideal. Here are a few inspiring examples of how it's being put into practice:

Bhutan's Gross National Happiness: This tiny Himalayan nation has long championed the concept of Gross National Happiness (GNH), prioritizing the well-being of its citizens over purely economic growth.
New Zealand's Well-being Budget: New Zealand made headlines by becoming the first country to introduce a "well-being budget," allocating resources based on how they contribute to the overall well-being of its people.
Iceland's Well-being Economy: Iceland is leading the way in creating a "well-being economy," prioritizing work-life balance, gender equality, and environmental sustainability.

The Path Forward: Challenges and Opportunities

While the movement to embrace well-being metrics is gaining momentum, there are still hurdles to overcome. Measuring well-being can be complex, and there's no one-size-fits-all solution. But with advancements in data collection and analysis, coupled with growing public awareness and political will, the future looks promising.

Imagine a world where governments prioritize policies that promote happiness, health, and sustainability alongside economic growth. A world where progress is measured not just by how much we produce, but by how well we live. This is the promise of the "beyond GDP" movement – a movement that has the potential to transform our economies and our societies for the better.

Ever Wonder Why You Buy That Extra Latte? It's Not Just Caffeine, It's Behavioral Economics!

Let's face it, we humans aren't always the most rational creatures. We splurge on things we don't need, procrastinate on important tasks, and sometimes make financial decisions that leave us scratching our heads. But what if we could harness these quirks and "nudge" ourselves towards a brighter financial future? That's where the magic of behavioral economics comes in.

Think of it like this: imagine your brain is a mischievous puppy, full of energy and easily distracted. Traditional economics assumes we're all perfectly trained pups, always obeying the commands of logic and reason. But behavioral economics knows better. It understands that our inner puppies need a little guidance, a gentle nudge in the right direction.

Decoding the Quirks of Your Mind

Behavioral economics dives deep into the psychology behind our choices, revealing fascinating insights:

Present Bias: The "Treat Yourself" Trap: We crave instant gratification, like that tempting latte, even if it means sacrificing long-term savings goals. It's like the puppy choosing a belly rub now over a delicious bone later.

Loss Aversion: The Fear of Missing Out: We hate losing more than we love winning. This fear can make us stick to the familiar, even when taking a calculated risk could lead to greater gains. Our inner puppy clings to its old chew toy, afraid to try a new one.

Framing Effects: The Power of Presentation: The way information is presented can dramatically sway our decisions. Imagine two dog treats: one labeled "90% fat-free" and the other "10% fat." Which one sounds more appealing? Our puppy, like us, falls for clever marketing.

Nudging Our Way to Financial Well-being

So how can we use these insights to improve our financial lives? Here are a few "nudges" to get us started:

Gamify Your Finances: Turn saving and budgeting into a fun game with apps and challenges. It's like teaching your puppy new tricks with rewards and positive reinforcement.
Automate Your Savings: Set up automatic transfers to your savings account. This way, you'll consistently save without even thinking about it. It's like having an invisible fence that keeps your puppy from straying from the yard.
Set Achievable Goals: Break down big financial goals into smaller, more manageable steps. Celebrate each milestone along the way. It's like taking your puppy on a long walk, with plenty of rest stops and treats to keep them motivated.
Simplify Your Choices: Too many options can lead to decision paralysis. Streamline your finances by consolidating accounts and minimizing unnecessary financial products. It's like giving your puppy a few carefully chosen toys instead of overwhelming them with a whole toy store.

The Future of Nudging

As technology advances, we can expect even more personalized and effective nudges. Imagine AI-powered financial assistants that understand our individual biases and offer tailored guidance. It's like having a personal dog trainer for your finances!

Behavioral economics reminds us that we're not perfect, but we can learn to harness our quirks to achieve our financial goals. So, the next time you're tempted by that extra latte, remember your inner puppy and ask yourself: "Is this a treat I truly want, or am I just falling for a momentary urge?" By understanding our biases and embracing the power of nudges, we can all pave the way for a more secure and fulfilling financial future.

The Unspoken Toll: How Inflation Whispers Despair to Vulnerable Minds

Imagine a world where the price tags on everyday items seem to have a life of their own, constantly creeping higher. For many, this is the reality of inflation, a silent thief that erodes the value of hard-earned money and amplifies existing inequalities. While its impact on the economy is widely discussed, the insidious effects of inflation on mental health, particularly among vulnerable populations, often remain hidden in the shadows.

The Crushing Weight of Uncertainty

Inflation doesn't just lighten wallets; it weighs heavily on minds. The relentless rise in the cost of living can transform everyday necessities into sources of constant anxiety. Imagine the stress of a parent struggling to put food on the table, or an elderly person on a fixed income forced to choose between medication and heat. This financial strain can trigger a cascade of mental health challenges:

A Symphony of Stress: The persistent worry about making ends meet can keep the body in a constant state of "fight-or-flight," leading to chronic stress, anxiety, and even physical ailments like insomnia and digestive issues.
The Shadow of Depression: As financial struggles drag on, feelings of hopelessness and helplessness can take root, paving the way for depression. This can manifest as a loss of interest in once-enjoyed activities, social withdrawal, and a pervasive sense of despair.
Desperate Measures: In extreme cases, the overwhelming burden of financial strain and mental anguish can lead to suicidal thoughts and behaviors.

Who Bears the Brunt?

While inflation affects everyone, its impact is not felt equally. Vulnerable populations, already facing significant challenges, are disproportionately affected:

Families on the Brink: For low-income families, even a small increase in prices can push them over the edge. Parents may be forced to make impossible choices between essentials, leading to immense guilt and stress.

The Forgotten Elderly: Many seniors live on fixed incomes that lose their purchasing power as prices rise. This can lead to social isolation, food insecurity, and a decline in physical and mental health.

Those Living with Disabilities: Individuals with disabilities often face higher medical costs and limited employment opportunities. Inflation can exacerbate these challenges, leading to financial instability and increased risk of mental health issues.

A Lifeline in the Storm: Strengthening Social Safety Nets

Social safety nets are the buffers that protect vulnerable populations from the harshest blows of economic hardship. These programs, ranging from unemployment benefits to food assistance, can be the difference between despair and resilience in the face of inflation.

Economic Empowerment: Direct cash transfers, housing subsidies, and food assistance programs can provide immediate relief, ensuring that basic needs are met and reducing the stress of financial insecurity.

Mental Health Support: Expanding access to affordable mental healthcare services is crucial. This includes increasing funding for community mental health centers, reducing the stigma associated with seeking help, and ensuring mental health coverage in insurance plans.

A Call to Action: Investing in Humanity

Addressing the mental health consequences of inflation requires a multifaceted approach:

Bolstering Social Programs: Governments must prioritize funding for social safety nets, ensuring that these programs are adequately resourced to meet the growing needs of vulnerable populations.

Expanding Access: Eligibility criteria for social programs should be reviewed and expanded to include those who are struggling but may not meet current requirements.

Breaking Barriers: Access to mental healthcare must be improved by reducing costs, increasing the availability of providers, and addressing the stigma that prevents many from seeking help.

Early Intervention: Investing in preventative measures and early intervention programs can help identify and support individuals at risk before their mental health deteriorates.

A World Where Everyone Thrives

The impact of inflation extends far beyond economic statistics; it touches the lives and minds of individuals and families. By investing in robust social safety nets and prioritizing mental health support, we can build a society where everyone has the opportunity to thrive, even in the face of economic challenges. Let us not allow inflation to become a silent epidemic of despair, but rather an opportunity to strengthen our commitment to compassion and social justice.

A World of Wellbeing: How Nations Are Battling the Mental Health Blues of Inflation

The global economy is a bit like a rollercoaster right now, with inflation throwing everyone for a loop. And just like a rollercoaster, it can make your stomach churn and your head spin. But fear not, fellow riders! Countries around the world are getting creative in finding ways to keep their citizens mentally healthy during these turbulent times. Let's take a peek at some of their innovative approaches:

1. Australia: Nipping it in the Bud (and the Budget)

Imagine a world where mental health support is as easy to access as a trip to the doctor. That's the vibe in Australia, where they're all about prevention and early intervention. They have organizations like Beyond blue, a digital haven offering online resources and support for those grappling with anxiety and depression. It's like a virtual hug when you need it most. And for the younger crowd, there's Headspace, a youth mental health foundation offering a safe space and crucial support for young people. Add to that their Medicare-subsidized mental health care, and you've got a recipe for mental wellbeing, even when the cost of living is sky-high.

2. Canada: Stronger Together

Canada knows that a problem shared is a problem halved. They're tackling the mental health fallout of inflation by fostering strong communities and support networks. Think community mental health centers that act as hubs of support, offering counseling, crisis assistance, and a helping hand to navigate resources. They also champion peer support programs, connecting people with shared experiences, because sometimes, a listening ear from someone who "gets it" is all you need. And let's not forget their social inclusion initiatives, like affordable housing and income support, because a stable foundation is crucial for mental wellbeing.

3. Finland: Happy Workers, Healthy Minds

Finland, the land of saunas and sisu (that gritty Finnish determination), understands that a happy workplace equals a healthy mind. They've made workplace mental health promotion a national priority. Finnish employers are legally bound to provide occupational health services, including mental health support. Imagine having access to stress management programs and mindfulness training right at your workplace! Plus, Finnish workplaces champion open communication, encouraging employees to talk about their mental health without fear of judgment.

4. Japan: Navigating the Job Jungle with Support

Japan has weathered its share of economic storms, and they've learned a thing or two about dealing with job insecurity. They offer specialized mental health services for job seekers, recognizing that unemployment can be a real blow to one's mental state. Public awareness campaigns featuring celebrities talking about their own mental health struggles help to break down stigma and encourage people to seek help. And a robust social safety net provides a much-needed cushion during tough times.

5. United Kingdom: Baking Mental Wellbeing into the Economic Pie

The UK is taking a holistic approach, weaving mental health considerations into its economic policies. Their "Thriving at Work" initiative encourages employers to create mentally healthy workplaces. They're also investing heavily in mental health services and conducting mental health impact assessments before implementing new policies. It's like a mental health check-up for the economy!

The Global Takeaway

These international examples show us that there's no one-size-fits-all solution. But there are common threads: early intervention, community support, workplace wellbeing, tackling job insecurity, and integrating mental health into economic policies. By learning from each other and adapting these approaches to their unique contexts, countries can create a world where everyone can thrive, even when the economic rollercoaster takes a dip.

Chapter 14: Mental Healthcare in an Inflationary World

Unmasking Mental Health: A Tapestry of Resilience

Imagine a vibrant tapestry, woven with threads of diverse experiences, where every color represents a unique individual. Yet, some threads are frayed, their brilliance dimmed by the weight of mental health disparities. These are the threads of low-income and marginalized communities, often silenced and overlooked.

The Unseen Shackles: Barriers to Mental Wellness

For these communities, the pursuit of mental well-being is like navigating a labyrinth with invisible walls. Financial constraints cast long shadows, making therapy and medication seem like distant luxuries. The scarcity of mental health professionals in their neighborhoods leaves them stranded in a desert of unmet needs.

Stigma, like a venomous whisper, coils around their hearts, discouraging them from seeking help. They grapple with cultural nuances that mainstream providers often miss, their pain lost in translation. The journey to a distant clinic becomes an odyssey when affordable transportation is a mirage.

Threads of Hope: Weaving a New Narrative

But amidst these challenges, sparks of innovation ignite. Community-based programs bloom like wildflowers, bringing mental health services directly to those who need them most. Telehealth bridges geographical gaps, offering virtual lifelines to remote corners.

Integrated care models weave mental health into the fabric of primary care, creating a safety net that catches those who might otherwise slip through the cracks. Peer support groups emerge as sanctuaries of shared understanding, where lived experiences illuminate the path to recovery.

Culturally adapted interventions, like masterfully crafted tapestries, honor the unique patterns of diverse communities, ensuring that healing resonates with their deepest values.

A Call to Action: Reweaving the Fabric of Care

Yet, individual threads alone cannot mend the entire tapestry. We need a collective loom, powered by policy and advocacy, to weave a more equitable future. Increased funding for mental health services is the warp that strengthens the foundation.

Expanding insurance coverage is the weft that interlaces affordability, ensuring that cost is no longer a barrier. Strengthening the mental health workforce adds vibrant new threads, diversifying the tapestry with skilled and compassionate providers.

Reducing stigma, like sunlight, dispels the shadows, empowering individuals to seek help without shame. Promoting early intervention and prevention is like weaving protective threads, safeguarding mental well-being from the start.

A Tapestry of Resilience: Embracing Our Shared Humanity

Let us embrace the intricate beauty of our collective tapestry, recognizing that every thread, every individual, deserves the chance to shine brightly. By addressing the barriers to mental healthcare for low-income and marginalized communities, we not only mend the frayed edges but also enrich the entire tapestry with resilience, compassion, and hope.

This is a call to action, a plea to reweave the fabric of care, ensuring that mental well-being is a right, not a privilege, accessible to all. For in the tapestry of humanity, every thread is precious, every story deserves to be heard, and every life has the potential to flourish.

Feeling the Pinch: Why Our Minds Need Check-ups Too

We all know that regular doctor visits are important for our physical health, but what about our mental well-being? Especially when times get tough, like when the economy takes a downturn and money worries start creeping in, our mental health can really take a hit. It's like a hidden weight on our shoulders, impacting everything from our sleep to our relationships.

Think of it this way: just like a car needs a tune-up to keep running smoothly, our minds need check-ups too. Early detection of mental health struggles, like anxiety or depression, is key. It's much easier to address a small problem before it becomes a major breakdown.

The Mind-Money Connection

When money's tight, stress levels skyrocket. We lose sleep worrying about bills, we might isolate ourselves from friends and family due to shame or lack of funds for social activities, and relationships can become strained. It's a vicious cycle that can leave us feeling powerless and hopeless.

Why Early Detection Matters

Imagine a small crack in a bridge. Ignore it, and it could eventually lead to a catastrophic collapse. The same goes for our mental health. Untreated issues can spiral, impacting not just our emotional well-being but also our physical health, our jobs, and even our relationships.

Mental Health Check-ups: A Lifeline in Primary Care

Here's the good news: integrating mental health screenings into routine doctor visits can be a game-changer. It's like adding a crucial diagnostic tool to the doctor's toolkit. This means:

Easier Access: No need to find a separate therapist or navigate the often-confusing mental health system. It's all right there at your family doctor's office.
Breaking the Stigma: By making mental health checks routine, we normalize the conversation and chip away at the stigma that prevents so many people from seeking help.
Early Intervention: Catching issues early means faster intervention and better chances of recovery.

Real-World Success Stories

This isn't just a theory. Studies have shown that routine mental health screenings in primary care led to:

More accurate diagnoses of depression.
Fewer trips to the emergency room for mental health crises.
Better overall health outcomes and lower healthcare costs.
Taking Charge of Our Mental Well-being

Let's face it, life can throw curveballs. Economic uncertainty is a reality for many of us. But by advocating for routine mental health screenings in primary care, we can empower ourselves and our communities to prioritize mental well-being. It's time to break the stigma, seek support, and build a healthier, more resilient future.

The Inflation Blues: How Healthcare Heroes Can Heal Minds and Wallets

Imagine a world where your paycheck shrinks faster than a sweater in the wash. That's the reality for many facing inflation's relentless squeeze. It's not just about tightening belts; it's about tightening chests, as anxiety and despair creep in.

But fear not! Our healthcare heroes are stepping up, armed with empathy and a whole new toolkit to mend not just bodies, but battered spirits too.

Beyond Band-Aids: The Mind-Wallet Connection

Think of inflation as a silent thief, robbing people of more than just buying power. It steals peace of mind, leaving behind a trail of stress, shattered dreams, and even broken families.

The Worry Spiral: Prices skyrocket, and suddenly, putting food on the table feels like climbing a mountain. Sleepless nights become the norm, as worries about bills and job security swirl endlessly.
The Hope Drain: When making ends meet feels impossible, a dark cloud of hopelessness can descend. Depression sets in, making it hard to find joy, even in the little things.

The Breaking Point: For some, the pressure cooker of financial strain explodes into substance abuse or domestic violence.

Healthcare Warriors to the Rescue!

Doctors, nurses, therapists – they're all becoming frontline warriors in the battle against inflation's mental health fallout. But this isn't your grandma's healthcare; it's a new era of compassionate care that understands the deep link between our minds and our wallets.

Superpowers for the Modern Healer

Economic X-Ray Vision: These healthcare heroes can see beyond the symptoms to the root causes, understanding how inflation, inequality, and joblessness wreak havoc on mental well-being.

Cultural Decoder Ring: They speak the language of empathy, recognizing that different cultures experience and express distress in unique ways.

Trauma-Informed Touch: They know that financial hardship can be traumatic, and offer care that heals instead of re-wounding.

Financial First Aid: They're equipped to offer basic money management advice and connect people with resources to regain control of their finances.

Stress-Busting Arsenal: They teach coping skills like mindfulness and relaxation techniques, empowering people to navigate the storm.

Advocates for Change: They don't just treat the symptoms; they raise their voices for policies that tackle the root causes of economic hardship.

Walking the Walk: Care that Truly Cares

This new breed of healthcare professional understands that one size doesn't fit all. They meet people where they are, offering:

Language that Connects: Services in your mother tongue, so you feel heard and understood.

Beliefs that Matter: Respect for your cultural values and how they shape your view of mental health.

Practices that Resonate: Treatments that incorporate your cultural traditions and beliefs.

Resources that Empower: Connections to support systems that are relevant to your culture and economic situation.
Stigma-Smashing: Challenging the shame and silence that often surround mental health, particularly in certain cultures.

Real Stories, Real Impact

A Single Mom's Struggle: Overwhelmed by soaring prices and the struggle to feed her children, she finds a lifeline in a healthcare provider who understands the unique challenges of single parenthood in poverty.
A Refugee Family's Journey: Fleeing conflict only to face the harsh realities of financial hardship in a new land, they find solace in a culturally sensitive therapist who helps them heal from trauma and rebuild their lives.

The Bottom Line: Hope on the Horizon

Inflation may be a formidable foe, but with these compassionate, skilled healthcare professionals on our side, we can weather the storm. They're not just patching us up; they're empowering us to thrive, even in the face of economic adversity. Because true healthcare is about more than just treating illnesses; it's about nurturing resilience, fostering hope, and ensuring that everyone, regardless of their background or bank balance, has the chance to live a mentally healthy life.

The Mind's New Machine: A Technological Renaissance in Mental Healthcare

Imagine a world where the stigma of mental health melts away, replaced by accessible and personalized care tailored to individual needs. This isn't a utopian dream, but a reality taking shape through the transformative power of technology.

Artificial Intelligence: The Mind's New Best Friend

AI is no longer a futuristic fantasy; it's revolutionizing mental healthcare with its ability to analyze vast amounts of data and provide insights beyond human capability.

Early Detection & Diagnosis: Imagine an AI system that scans social media posts, not to sell you products, but to detect early signs of depression or anxiety. This is the power of AI to identify those at risk before conditions escalate.
Personalized Treatment: Forget one-size-fits-all therapy. AI can analyze your unique characteristics and preferences to create a treatment plan just for you, ensuring the most effective care. Think of it as having a personal mental wellness coach in your pocket.
24/7 Support: Struggling at 2 AM? AI-powered chatbots offer immediate support and coping strategies, ensuring you're never alone in your mental health journey.

Virtual Reality: Stepping into Healing Worlds

VR isn't just for gaming anymore; it's creating immersive experiences that transport patients to healing environments.

Conquering Fears: Afraid of public speaking? VR can simulate real-life scenarios, allowing you to practice and overcome your anxieties in a safe space.
Finding Inner Peace: Escape to serene virtual beaches or forests, where guided meditation and relaxation techniques wash away stress and promote mindfulness.
Pain Management: VR can distract from chronic pain by immersing you in engaging experiences, offering a non-invasive complement to traditional pain management.

Beyond AI & VR: A Plethora of Digital Tools

Mobile Apps: Mental wellness apps provide on-the-go support, from mood tracking to mindfulness exercises, empowering you to take control of your mental health.
Wearable Tech: Smartwatches and fitness trackers can monitor your physiological data, providing insights into your mental well-being and prompting timely interventions.
Teletherapy: Access therapy from anywhere in the world, breaking down geographical barriers and increasing access to care for those in remote or underserved areas.

Gamification: Games aren't just for fun; they can make learning coping skills interactive and enjoyable, increasing engagement and motivation.

Challenges & Ethical Considerations

As we embrace this technological revolution, it's crucial to address potential challenges:

Data Privacy: Protecting sensitive mental health data is paramount. Robust security measures are essential to prevent breaches and maintain patient trust.
Accessibility: Not everyone has equal access to technology. Bridging the digital divide is crucial to ensure equitable access to digital mental health resources.
Ethical AI: AI algorithms must be developed responsibly to avoid bias and discrimination, ensuring fairness and transparency.
Clinical Validation: Digital tools should undergo rigorous testing to demonstrate their effectiveness and safety, providing patients with reliable and validated solutions.

The Future of Mental Healthcare: A Tech-Enabled Horizon

Technology is not meant to replace human connection, but to enhance it. The future holds even more exciting possibilities:

Integrated Solutions: Imagine AI, VR, and wearables working together to create comprehensive and personalized mental healthcare experiences.
Predictive Analytics: AI could predict mental health crises by analyzing individual risk factors, allowing for timely interventions and preventative care.
Enhanced Personalization: Treatments will become even more tailored to individual needs and preferences, maximizing effectiveness and patient satisfaction.
In conclusion, technology is ushering in a new era of mental healthcare, one where stigma is replaced by understanding, and barriers to care are broken down by innovation. By embracing these advancements responsibly and ethically, we can create a future where everyone has the opportunity to thrive in mind, body, and spirit.

Chapter 15: The Double Bind

The Weight of the World: When Inflation and Climate Change Collide

Aisha clutches her electricity bill, the numbers blurring through her tears. It's not just the cost of keeping the lights on; it's the empty space in the fridge where her son's favorite yogurt used to be, the worn-out shoes she can't afford to replace. Outside, the wind howls, a constant reminder of the rising tides that threaten to swallow her coastal town whole. Aisha feels like she's drowning, not in water, but in a sea of anxieties – financial worries crashing against the fear of a changing climate.

This is the reality of compound crises. It's not just about numbers; it's about the human stories behind them. It's about the parents who lie awake at night, calculating how to stretch their shrinking budgets, the farmers watching their crops wither under relentless droughts, the young people inheriting a world on the brink.

Inflation: The Silent Thief

Inflation isn't just an economic term; it's a thief that steals joy, stability, and hope. It whispers doubts in your ear: "Will I be able to feed my family? Will I lose my home? Will I ever feel secure again?" It's a constant pressure, a weight on your chest that makes it hard to breathe.

Imagine a musician who can no longer afford strings for their guitar, a teacher skipping meals to pay for school supplies, a single mother choosing between rent and medication. These are the faces of inflation, the human cost of rising prices.

Climate Change: The Unfolding Disaster

Climate change isn't just about melting glaciers and rising sea levels; it's about the fear in the eyes of a child watching wildfires rage across their homeland. It's about the farmer's despair as their fields turn to dust, the fisherman's empty nets as the ocean's bounty dwindles.

It's a creeping dread, a sense of impending loss that can manifest as panic attacks in crowded spaces, nightmares of flooded cities, or a deep, pervasive sadness for the future. This "eco-anxiety" is a growing phenomenon, particularly among young people who feel they're inheriting a planet in peril.

The Crushing Weight of Compound Crises

When these two giants – inflation and climate change – collide, the impact can be devastating. It's like being caught in a perfect storm, battered by waves of economic hardship and environmental uncertainty. This can lead to a sense of overwhelm, a feeling of being trapped in a system that's spiraling out of control.

"It's like I'm being squeezed from all sides," says Maria, a single mother in a rural community. "I'm worried about putting food on the table, and I'm terrified of the next wildfire season. I feel like I'm constantly on edge, waiting for the next disaster to strike."

Finding Resilience in the Storm

But even in the darkest of times, the human spirit finds ways to shine through. Resilience isn't about ignoring the pain; it's about acknowledging it and finding ways to cope, to heal, to move forward.

Sharing the Burden: Connecting with others who understand your struggles can be a lifeline. Support groups, community gatherings, and online forums can provide a space to share fears, offer encouragement, and build a sense of solidarity.

Finding Solace in Nature: Even as the natural world faces unprecedented challenges, it can also offer solace and healing. Spending time in nature, whether it's a walk in the park or a weekend camping trip, can reduce stress, boost mood, and reconnect us to the beauty and resilience of the Earth.

Turning Anxiety into Action: Channeling eco-anxiety into positive action can be empowering. Joining a climate action group, volunteering for environmental causes, or simply making sustainable choices in your daily life can help you feel like you're making a difference.

Creative Expression: Art, music, writing, and other forms of creative expression can be powerful tools for processing emotions, finding meaning, and building resilience. Expressing your anxieties through art can help you transform fear into something beautiful and meaningful.

A Call to Hope and Action

The challenges we face are immense, but so is our capacity for hope, creativity, and collective action. We can't afford to succumb to despair. We need to embrace our interconnectedness, support each other, and work together to create a more just and sustainable future.

This isn't just about surviving; it's about thriving. It's about finding ways to live meaningful, fulfilling lives, even in the face of uncertainty. It's about rediscovering our connection to nature, to each other, and to the enduring human spirit that has overcome countless challenges throughout history.

The Weight of a Melting World: Navigating Eco-Anxiety and Climate Grief

The air hangs heavy, not just with humidity, but with a sense of foreboding. The newsfeeds are a relentless scroll of wildfires, floods, and extinctions. It's not just the polar bears anymore; it's the bees, the birds, the forests we played in as children, all seeming to slip through our fingers like sand. This is the age of eco-anxiety, where the weight of a melting world presses down on our souls.

Imagine carrying a backpack that gets heavier with each passing day. Inside are the worries – the creeping dread of rising sea levels, the guilt of a carbon footprint, the despair at the inaction of those in power. This is the burden of eco-anxiety, a chronic fear for the future of our planet, a constant knot in the stomach that refuses to unwind.

But there's another weight, a deeper ache in the chest. It's the grief for what we've already lost – the bleached coral reefs, the silenced birdsong, the landscapes transformed beyond recognition. This is climate grief, a mourning for the Earth as we knew it, a longing for a wholeness that seems irretrievably broken.

It's like watching a loved one slowly succumb to illness. We rage against the unfairness, we bargain with fate, we sink into despair. We may even experience a kind of survivor's guilt, wondering why we are allowed to continue living while entire ecosystems vanish.

This emotional toll is real. It manifests in sleepless nights, panic attacks, and a pervasive sense of hopelessness. It can strain relationships, as we struggle to connect with those who seem oblivious to the crisis unfolding around us. It can even lead to a loss of identity, as the places and landscapes that define us disappear beneath the waves or wither under a scorching sun.

Think of the Indigenous communities witnessing the melting of ancient glaciers, their cultural heritage literally dissolving before their eyes. Or the farmers watching their crops fail year after year, their livelihoods and way of life crumbling into dust. These are not abstract concepts; they are the lived experiences of millions around the world.

But amidst the despair, there are glimmers of hope. Like seeds sprouting in scorched earth, resilience and resistance are taking root.

We are finding solace in nature, reconnecting with the Earth's rhythms and drawing strength from its enduring beauty. We are building communities of support, sharing our fears and grief, and finding collective strength in shared purpose. We are channeling our anxiety into action, demanding change from our leaders, and making conscious choices to lessen our impact on the planet.

We are learning to practice mindfulness, to find moments of peace amidst the chaos, to cultivate gratitude for the wonders that remain. We are rediscovering our connection to something larger than ourselves, finding meaning in the fight for a livable future.

This is not an easy journey. There will be days when the weight of the world feels unbearable. But we are not alone. Together, we can navigate the turbulent waters of eco-anxiety and climate grief, finding strength in our shared humanity and our unwavering love for this fragile planet we call home.

The World is Shaking, But We Are Not Broken

Remember that feeling of riding a roller coaster? The stomach-churning climb, the sudden drops, the exhilarating twists and turns? That's 2024, my friend. Climate change is throwing heatwaves and floods our way. Political tensions are simmering. The economy? Well, let's just say it's playing hide-and-seek with our wallets.

It's enough to make you want to burrow under the covers and wait for the sunnier days promised in those old sci-fi movies. But here's the thing: we humans, we're surprisingly good at weathering storms.

Resilience: Not Just Bouncing Back, But Bouncing Forward

Resilience isn't about ignoring the chaos. It's about looking it square in the eye and saying, "Okay, world, you threw a curveball. Now watch me hit it out of the park."

Think of it like a tree in a hurricane. It bends, it sways, it might even lose a few branches. But its roots hold strong, and it keeps reaching for the sunlight. That's us. We might get knocked down, but we get back up, stronger and wiser.

Your Resilience Toolkit: More Than Just Duct Tape and Positive Thinking

Embrace the Wobble: Remember learning to ride a bike? All those wobbly starts, scraped knees, and near-misses? You didn't give up, did you? You kept pedaling, kept adjusting, and eventually, you were flying down the street, wind in your hair. That's the power of a growth mindset.
Find Your Tribe: We're not meant to go it alone. Connect with your people – family, friends, that quirky book club you joined. Sharing laughter, tears, and a pot of strong coffee can make even the toughest challenges feel a little less daunting.
Breathe. Just Breathe: When the world feels like a runaway train, take a moment to just be. Close your eyes, feel the ground beneath your

feet, listen to the rhythm of your breath. Mindfulness isn't about emptying your mind; it's about finding stillness in the storm.
Unleash Your Inner Artist: Paint, write, sing, dance, build a miniature replica of the Eiffel Tower out of toothpicks – whatever floats your creative boat. Expressing yourself can be incredibly healing and help you find meaning in the midst of chaos.

From Feeling Overwhelmed to Taking Action

It's easy to get paralyzed by the sheer scale of global challenges. But remember this: every ripple starts with a single drop.

Be a Changemaker: Support organizations doing good in the world. Volunteer your time. Speak up for what you believe in. Even small actions can create a wave of change.
Connect the Dots: Talk to people with different perspectives. Listen. Learn. Challenge your own assumptions. We're all in this together, and finding solutions requires open minds and open hearts.
Choose Hope: Yes, the world is messy. But it's also full of incredible beauty, kindness, and resilience. Focus on the good. Celebrate the wins. Believe in the power of humanity to create a better future.

We're Not Just Passengers on This Ride

We're the navigators, the engineers, the artists of our own lives. And even though the road ahead might be bumpy, we have the power to steer towards a brighter horizon. So, buckle up, hold on tight, and let's ride this wave together.

Our Shared Earth: A Tapestry of Action

Imagine our planet as a vast, intricate tapestry. Each thread represents an individual, a community, an action. When woven together, these threads create a vibrant picture of resilience, innovation, and hope in the face of the climate crisis.

The Power of We: Communities as Catalysts for Change

Think of your local community as a microcosm of the world. Within it lies the power to spark change, to nurture solutions, and to build a more sustainable future.

Unearthing Local Treasures: Every community holds unique knowledge about its vulnerabilities and strengths. By engaging in open dialogues, sharing stories, and brainstorming ideas, we can collectively identify the most effective ways to adapt to and mitigate climate change at the local level.
Seeds of Change: Community gardens bursting with fresh produce, solar panels glinting in the sun, bike lanes weaving through bustling streets – these are just a few examples of how communities can take concrete steps towards sustainability.
Stronger Together: When we work together, we create a safety net, a support system that empowers us to face challenges head-on and emerge stronger.

A Global Chorus: Raising Our Voices for Systemic Change

While local action is vital, we must also address the root causes of climate change at the systemic level. This requires us to amplify our voices and demand bold action from our leaders.

The Power of the Pen: A handwritten letter to a representative, a carefully crafted email to a senator – these seemingly small acts can have a ripple effect, influencing policy decisions and shaping the future.
Championing the Cause: Supporting organizations dedicated to climate action, whether through volunteering or donations, is an investment in a healthier planet.
Digital Dialogue: Social media platforms have become powerful tools for raising awareness, mobilizing support, and holding decision-makers accountable.

Every Action Counts: Weaving Our Threads into the Tapestry

The climate crisis demands that we all become weavers of change. Here are a few ways to contribute to the tapestry:

Become a Climate Connoisseur: Immerse yourself in the science, explore the impacts, and discover the solutions. Knowledge is power.
Find Your Tribe: Connect with local climate action groups, share your passion, and learn from others.
Vote with Your Conscience: Support candidates who prioritize environmental sustainability and have a strong track record on climate action.
Green Your Lifestyle: Embrace sustainable habits, from reducing energy consumption to choosing eco-friendly products.
Spark Conversations: Talk about climate change with your friends, family, and colleagues. Spread awareness and inspire action.

Together, We Can Rewrite the Narrative

The climate crisis is a daunting challenge, but it is not insurmountable. By embracing collective action, by weaving our individual threads into a tapestry of resilience and hope, we can create a future where both humanity and nature thrive. Let's rewrite the narrative, together.

Chapter 16: The Metaverse

Stepping into the Metaverse: A New Frontier for Mental Well-being

Imagine a world where you can conquer your fears, connect with others, and find solace, all without leaving the comfort of your home. This is the promise of the metaverse, a digital realm that's opening up exciting new possibilities for mental health support and therapy.

Virtual Reality: A Safe Haven for the Mind

Think of VR as a digital sanctuary, a place where you can face your anxieties and practice social skills in a safe, controlled environment. Whether it's public speaking jitters or the overwhelming fear of a crowded room, VR allows you to confront these challenges at your own pace, building resilience and confidence along the way.

Social Connection: Bridging the Gap

In a world that can often feel isolating, VR provides a lifeline for social connection. Imagine joining a support group where you can share experiences with others who truly understand, or stepping into a vibrant virtual world where you can forge meaningful connections with people from all walks of life.

Beyond the Screen: Real-World Benefits

The impact of VR extends far beyond the digital realm. Studies have shown that VR therapy can lead to significant improvements in social anxiety, PTSD, and even depression. By immersing individuals in realistic simulations, VR empowers them to develop coping mechanisms and regain control of their lives.

A Glimpse into the Future

As VR technology continues to evolve, we can expect even more innovative applications for mental health. From virtual nature retreats that soothe the soul to personalized therapeutic experiences tailored to individual needs, the metaverse holds the potential to revolutionize the way we approach mental well-being.

Important Note: While VR offers incredible promise, it's important to remember that it's not a replacement for professional help. If you're struggling with a mental health condition, seeking guidance from a qualified mental health professional is crucial.

Let's embrace the metaverse as a powerful tool for healing and connection, a place where we can explore the limitless potential of the human mind and discover new pathways to well-being.

The Siren Song of the Screen: When Virtual Worlds Become Too Real

Imagine a world where the grass is always greener, the sun always shines, and your wildest dreams are just a click away. That's the allure of virtual escapism, a seductive siren song that can pull us into a digital ocean of endless possibilities. But like the sailors of old, we must be wary of crashing against the rocks of addiction, dissociation, and a blurred sense of reality.

Falling Down the Rabbit Hole: The Addictive Nature of Virtual Escape

Our brains are wired to seek pleasure and avoid pain. Virtual worlds offer a potent cocktail of dopamine-inducing rewards, from the thrill of victory in a game to the warm embrace of an online community. But when these virtual pleasures become our primary source of happiness, we risk falling into the clutches of addiction.

Think of it like this: you stumble upon a magical garden overflowing with delectable fruits. At first, you savor each bite, enjoying the novelty and sweetness. But soon, you find yourself craving only this fruit, neglecting the nourishment of real-world meals and relationships. Your once vibrant life begins to wither as you spend all your time in the garden, chasing an insatiable hunger.

Losing Yourself in the Looking Glass: Dissociation and Identity Confusion

Virtual worlds offer a chance to reinvent ourselves, to slip into new identities and explore uncharted territories. But when we spend too much time in these digital reflections, we risk losing sight of our true selves.

Imagine stepping through a looking glass into a world where you are a powerful warrior, a brilliant artist, or a charismatic leader. The longer you stay in this reflected reality, the more your real-world image begins to fade. You may start to feel like a stranger in your own life, disconnected from your body, your emotions, and your sense of self.

The Mirage of Perfection: Blurring the Lines Between Real and Virtual

Virtual worlds often present an idealized version of reality, where challenges are easily overcome and relationships are free from conflict. This can create a dangerous dissonance when we return to the messy, unpredictable world of flesh and blood.

Think of it like watching a movie where the hero always triumphs and the ending is always happy. After immersing yourself in this cinematic fantasy, real life can feel dull and disappointing. You may find yourself longing for the effortless victories and perfect relationships of the virtual world, leading to dissatisfaction and a sense of detachment from reality.

Finding the Balance: Navigating the Virtual Landscape with Awareness

Virtual worlds can be a source of joy, connection, and even personal growth. But like any powerful tool, they must be used with caution and awareness. Here are some tips for navigating the virtual landscape without losing your way:

Set Limits: Treat virtual worlds like a delicious dessert – enjoy it in moderation, but don't let it become your main course.

Prioritize Real-World Connections: Nurture your relationships with friends, family, and loved ones. These are the people who will be there for you when the virtual lights go out.

Embrace the Messiness of Reality: Real life is full of challenges and imperfections, but it's also where we find true meaning and connection. Don't let the pursuit of virtual perfection blind you to the beauty of the present moment.

Seek Support: If you find yourself struggling with virtual escapism, don't hesitate to reach out for help. There are people who care and resources available to guide you back to a healthy balance.

Remember: Virtual worlds can be a valuable part of our lives, but they should never replace the richness and complexity of the real world. By staying grounded in our true selves and prioritizing meaningful connections, we can enjoy the benefits of virtual experiences without losing sight of what truly matters.

> Imagine a world where everyone belongs.

The metaverse is no longer a futuristic fantasy; it's knocking at our door, promising to reshape how we connect, work, and play. But as we step into this uncharted territory, we must ensure it's built on a foundation of inclusivity, equity, and safety. This isn't just about technology; it's about weaving a digital tapestry where everyone feels welcome and empowered, regardless of their background, abilities, or identity.

Breaking Down Barriers: Access for All

Think of the metaverse as a bustling city. Everyone deserves a ticket to enter, but the cost of VR headsets, high-speed internet, and other necessities can be like an insurmountable toll booth. To bridge this digital divide, we need creative solutions:

Subsidized Hardware Programs: Imagine community centers equipped with VR technology, offering affordable access to those who need it most.

Digital Literacy Initiatives: What if we had workshops and online resources that demystified the metaverse, empowering individuals with the skills to navigate this new world confidently?

Accessibility Built-In: Imagine a metaverse where avatars are customizable, with features like haptic feedback for the visually impaired and real-time captioning for those with hearing difficulties.
Examples:

Meta's "Accessibility in the Metaverse" initiative is exploring hand tracking, voice control, and personalized avatars to make VR more inclusive.
Microsoft's Alt Space VR has incorporated screen reader compatibility and avatar customization options to enhance accessibility.

A Tapestry of Diversity: Representation Matters

The metaverse should be a vibrant reflection of our world's rich diversity, a place where everyone feels seen, heard, and valued. This means:

Diverse Avatars: Imagine a world where you can express your true self through your avatar, with a wide array of skin tones, body types, hairstyles, and cultural attire.
Inclusive Content Creation: Imagine stories and experiences created by people from all walks of life, offering diverse perspectives and challenging stereotypes.
Combatting Bias: Imagine AI-powered tools and community moderators working together to identify and address harmful biases and stereotypes, creating a safe and respectful environment.

Examples:

Ready Player Me allows users to create personalized avatars that can be used across various metaverse platforms, promoting self-expression.
The Black Metaverse is a community-driven initiative focused on creating spaces that celebrate Black culture and promote inclusivity.
Safety First: Building a Secure and Respectful Environment

Just like any city, the metaverse needs rules and safeguards to ensure everyone feels secure. This means:

Clear Community Guidelines: Imagine a metaverse with clear and enforced guidelines against harassment, hate speech, and other harmful behaviors.
Effective Moderation: Imagine AI-powered systems and human moderators working together to detect and address harmful content and interactions.
Support Systems: Imagine accessible reporting mechanisms and support systems for users who experience harassment or other issues.

Examples:

Meta's Horizon Worlds has implemented a "personal boundary" feature that prevents other avatars from getting too close and a reporting system for users to flag inappropriate behavior.
The Center for Democracy & Technology (CDT) is working to develop ethical guidelines and best practices for online safety and privacy in the metaverse.

Beyond the Basics: Additional Considerations

Age-Appropriate Content: The metaverse should offer content suitable for users of different ages, with appropriate safety measures in place for younger users.
Cultural Sensitivity: We need to design the metaverse with cultural sensitivity in mind, avoiding cultural appropriation and ensuring respect for diverse cultural values.
Data Privacy and Security: Protecting user data and privacy is paramount. Strong data security measures and transparent data privacy policies are essential.

Conclusion: Building a Metaverse for Everyone

Creating an inclusive and equitable metaverse is a shared responsibility. Developers, policymakers, educators, and users all have a role to play. By prioritizing access, representation, and safety, we can build a metaverse that truly reflects the best of humanity. Let's commit to creating a digital world where everyone feels welcome, empowered, and safe to explore their full potential.

The Metaverse: A Brave New World for Work and Social Connection (or a Mental Health Minefield?)

Hold onto your hats, folks, because we're diving headfirst into the metaverse – a digital wonderland where work, play, and socializing collide! It's a place where you can teleport to your office in pajamas, attend a virtual concert with friends across the globe, and even reinvent yourself with a snazzy new avatar. Sounds like a dream, right?

But before we get carried away with the metaverse hype, let's take a closer look at how this brave new world might impact our mental well-being, especially when real-world economic anxieties like inflation are looming large.

Work in the Metaverse: The Good, the Bad, and the Ugly

Imagine ditching your soul-crushing commute and stepping into a virtual office where creativity knows no bounds. That's the promise of work in the metaverse. But is it all sunshine and rainbows?

The Upsides:

Flexibility and Freedom: Say goodbye to rigid schedules and hello to work-life balance! In the metaverse, you can work from anywhere, anytime, and even wear that unicorn onesie you've been hiding in your closet.
Collaboration on Steroids: Forget boring conference calls. In the metaverse, you can brainstorm with colleagues in interactive virtual spaces, making teamwork more engaging and productive.
Innovation Unleashed: The metaverse is a playground for innovation, where you can experiment with virtual prototypes and bring your wildest ideas to life.

The Downsides:

The Blurred Lines of Work-Life Balance: When your office is just a virtual hop, skip, and a jump away, it can be hard to switch off and recharge.
The Loneliness of the Long-Distance Worker: While the metaverse connects us in new ways, it can also lead to social isolation and a lack of real-world human interaction.
Digital Burnout: Spending too much time in the metaverse can lead to digital fatigue, eye strain, and a feeling of being constantly "on."
Socializing in the Metaverse: A Double-Edged Sword

The metaverse opens up a world of possibilities for social connection, but it also comes with its own set of challenges.

The Upsides:

Global Connections: Forge friendships with people from all corners of the globe who share your passions.
Express Yourself: Create a unique avatar that reflects your true self or explore different facets of your personality.
New Experiences: Attend virtual concerts, art exhibitions, and even therapy sessions from the comfort of your own home.

The Downsides:

Cyberbullying and Online Harassment: The anonymity of the metaverse can embolden some individuals to engage in harmful behaviors.
Addiction and Escapism: The immersive nature of the metaverse can be addictive, leading some to neglect their real-life responsibilities.
Unrealistic Expectations: The curated and often idealized nature of virtual identities can fuel social comparison and feelings of inadequacy.

Inflation and the Metaverse: A Recipe for Mental Health Mayhem?

Economic anxieties like inflation can amplify the mental health risks associated with the metaverse. Financial stress can lead to increased social isolation, escapism, and a pressure to keep up with virtual trends.

Navigating the Metaverse: Tips for a Healthy Mind

So, how can we reap the benefits of the metaverse without falling prey to its potential pitfalls? Here are a few tips:

Set Boundaries: Establish clear boundaries between work and personal life, even in the virtual world.
Practice Mindfulness: Stay grounded in the present moment and avoid getting lost in the metaverse.
Build Strong Relationships: Nurture both online and offline relationships to combat social isolation.
Promote Digital Literacy: Educate yourself about the potential risks and benefits of the metaverse.
Advocate for Ethical Design: Demand metaverse platforms that prioritize user well-being and safety.

The Metaverse: A Work in Progress

The metaverse is still in its early stages of development, and it's up to us to shape its future. By being mindful of its potential impact on our mental health and taking steps to mitigate the risks, we can create a metaverse that enhances our lives, rather than detracts from them.

Let's build a metaverse that's not just a technological marvel, but a place where we can thrive both mentally and emotionally.

Chapter 17: Artificial Intelligence

The AI Revolution in Mental Health
Imagine a world where whispers of despair are caught before they become screams, where hidden patterns in our words and actions reveal the first signs of inner turmoil. This isn't science fiction; it's the promise of artificial intelligence in mental health.

Think of AI as a compassionate detective, tirelessly sifting through clues that might elude the human eye. It can analyze the nuances of our language, the subtle shifts in our online behavior, even the rhythm of our heartbeats, to paint a picture of our mental well-being.

Beyond the Surface:

The Silent Language of Data: AI algorithms can delve into our digital footprints – social media posts, emails, even our Google searches – to identify subtle shifts in mood and language that may signal distress. Imagine an AI companion that notices when your usually vibrant online persona turns quiet and withdrawn, offering a gentle nudge of support.
The Whispers in Our Voices: Our voices hold a wealth of information about our emotional state. AI can detect subtle tremors, changes in pitch, and pauses that might betray hidden anxieties or a deepening depression, alerting us to seek help before a crisis hits.
The Rhythm of Our Lives: Wearable sensors, like smartwatches, can track our sleep patterns, activity levels, and even heart rate variability. AI can analyze this data to identify subtle physiological changes that may precede a mental health episode, allowing for proactive intervention.

Real-World Heroes:

Ellie, the College Student: AI noticed Ellie's dwindling social media presence and increasingly negative posts. A concerned counselor reached out, offering support and resources, helping Ellie navigate a difficult period of anxiety.
John, the Veteran: AI detected subtle changes in John's voice, revealing a worsening of his PTSD symptoms. This early warning allowed for timely intervention and prevented a potential crisis.

Sarah, the New Mom: An AI-powered chatbot became Sarah's confidante, analyzing her conversations and recognizing the signs of postpartum depression. It offered personalized resources and connected her with a support group, reminding her that she wasn't alone.

A Future of Hope:

AI in mental health isn't about replacing human connection; it's about enhancing it. It's about empowering individuals and clinicians with powerful tools for early detection, personalized support, and proactive intervention. Imagine a future where:

AI assistants become our constant companions, offering support and guidance on our mental health journey.
Schools integrate AI-powered tools to identify students at risk, providing early intervention and preventing crises.
Workplaces utilize AI to promote mental well-being, creating a supportive environment where employees feel valued and understood.

The Human Element:

While AI offers incredible potential, it's crucial to remember that technology is only part of the solution. Human empathy, compassion, and understanding remain essential in the journey towards mental wellness. AI is a powerful tool, but it's the human connection that truly heals.

Let's embrace this technological revolution with open arms, using AI to create a world where mental health is prioritized, understood, and supported.

Mental Health Gets Personal: How AI is Revolutionizing Care

Imagine a world where mental health care isn't a one-size-fits-all approach, but a tailored journey guided by cutting-edge technology. That's the promise of Artificial Intelligence (AI). No more guessing games or generic treatments. AI is stepping in to offer personalized support, making mental wellness more attainable than ever.

AI: The Ultimate Mental Health Detective

Think of AI as a super-sleuth, meticulously analyzing mountains of data – from your medical records and wearable tech to your social media posts and even your voice! This deep dive helps identify hidden patterns and risk factors that humans might miss.

Early Intervention is Key: AI acts like an early warning system, detecting subtle signs of trouble, like a change in your voice or sleeping patterns. This allows for early intervention, potentially preventing a crisis down the road.

No More Treatment Roulette: Forget the trial-and-error approach to treatment. AI analyzes your unique data to predict which therapies or medications will be most effective for you.

Always-On Support: Need a pep talk at 2 AM? AI-powered chatbots and virtual assistants are available 24/7, offering support, coping strategies, and a listening ear whenever you need it.

Beyond the Chatbot: AI in Action

Virtual Reality Therapy: Step into a virtual world to safely confront your fears, practice social skills, or manage anxiety. AI-powered VR environments create realistic simulations, helping you build confidence and resilience in the real world.

Personalized Treatment Plans: AI platforms like Ginger and Meru Health use your data to create a customized care plan, connecting you with the right level of support, from self-guided resources to therapy sessions.

The Human Touch Still Matters

While AI is a game-changer, it's important to remember that technology is a tool, not a replacement for human connection. AI should work alongside therapists and healthcare professionals, enhancing their ability to provide compassionate, individualized care.

Challenges and Ethical Considerations

Of course, with any new technology, there are challenges to address:

Data Privacy: Protecting sensitive mental health information is paramount.
Algorithmic Bias: AI systems need to be carefully designed to avoid perpetuating existing biases in healthcare.
Ethical Use: We need to ensure AI is used responsibly and ethically in the context of mental health.

The Future is Personalized

AI is ushering in a new era of mental health care – one that is personalized, proactive, and accessible. As technology continues to evolve, we can expect even more innovative solutions that empower individuals to take control of their mental well-being. The future of mental health care is here, and it's looking brighter than ever.

The Algorithmic Therapist: Will AI Heal or Hinder?

Imagine a world where your therapist is available 24/7, never gets tired, and can analyze your speech patterns for subtle signs of distress you might not even be aware of. This is the promise of AI in mental healthcare – a digital shoulder to lean on, powered by algorithms and machine learning. But like a double-edged scalpel, this technology can cut both ways.

The Shadows of Bias

While AI holds immense potential, it's crucial to remember that algorithms are not neutral. They learn from the data they are fed, and if that data reflects existing societal biases, the AI will inherit them, like a digital echo chamber.

Think of an AI trained on data primarily from affluent, white communities. When confronted with a patient from a different background, with different cultural expressions of distress, the AI might misinterpret their symptoms, leading to misdiagnosis and potentially harmful treatment plans. This is like trying to understand a foreign language using only a dictionary – you might get the gist, but miss the nuances and cultural context.

Bridging the Digital Divide

Even with unbiased algorithms, access to AI-powered mental healthcare is another hurdle. Imagine a rural community with limited internet access or an elderly patient struggling with new technology. The very people who could benefit most from AI-powered support might be left behind, widening the existing gap in mental health services.

The Human Touch in a Digital World

The integration of AI in mental healthcare raises ethical questions that go beyond simple algorithms. Can a machine truly understand the complexities of human emotion? Can it provide the empathy and nuanced support that a human therapist can?

Perhaps the most promising approach lies in collaboration. Imagine AI as a tool that empowers therapists, not replaces them. AI could analyze data, identify patterns, and offer insights, while human therapists provide the empathy, understanding, and personalized guidance that machines cannot replicate.

A Call for Conscious Creation

The future of AI in mental healthcare hinges on our ability to address these challenges proactively. We need:

Diverse Data: Algorithms trained on data that reflects the beautiful tapestry of human experiences, ensuring that no one is left invisible.
Human-Centered Design: AI tools designed with empathy, considering the needs of diverse users, including those with limited digital literacy.
Ethical Frameworks: Guidelines that ensure AI is used responsibly, prioritizing patient well-being and avoiding harm.
The path forward is not about blindly embracing technology, but about wielding it with wisdom and compassion. By weaving together, the strengths of AI with the irreplaceable human touch, we can create a future where mental healthcare is more accessible, equitable, and effective for all.

The Mind's New Machine: A Human-AI Symphony in Mental Healthcare

Imagine a world where the whispers of the troubled mind are heard not just by human ears, but by the intricate algorithms of artificial intelligence. This isn't science fiction, but a blossoming reality where AI is stepping onto the stage of mental healthcare, not as a replacement, but as a partner in a harmonious duet with human clinicians.

This partnership is revolutionizing how we understand, diagnose, and treat mental health conditions. AI, with its tireless ability to sift through mountains of data and spot patterns invisible to the naked eye, is becoming a powerful ally in the fight against mental illness.

From Silent Observer to Active Participant

AI is no longer a passive bystander, merely analyzing data from the sidelines. It's stepping into the spotlight, engaging in active dialogue with patients through chatbots and virtual assistants. These digital companions offer immediate support, deliver personalized therapy, and even track a patient's progress with unwavering attention.

This allows human clinicians to shed some of their burden, freeing them to focus on the intricate nuances of the human mind that AI can't yet grasp. It's like having a tireless assistant who handles the routine tasks, allowing the maestro to concentrate on the symphony's most delicate and complex passages.

Bridging the Gap: Access, Affordability, and Acceptance

The traditional walls of the therapist's office are crumbling, replaced by digital doorways that open up access to mental healthcare like never before. AI-powered tools transcend geographical barriers and financial constraints, reaching those who need help the most, regardless of where they live or their ability to pay.

This is particularly crucial for younger generations, who are often more comfortable confiding in a digital companion than a human therapist. AI offers them anonymity, convenience, and a judgment-free space to explore their inner world.

The Ethical Tightrope: Navigating the Challenges

As AI's role expands, we must tread carefully, ensuring that this powerful technology is used responsibly and ethically. Data privacy, algorithmic bias, and the preservation of human connection are paramount concerns that must be addressed with unwavering vigilance.

AI should never become a substitute for human empathy and understanding. It's a tool, a powerful one, but still a tool that must be wielded with wisdom and compassion.

A Glimpse into the Future: Case Studies in Human-AI Collaboration

Woe bot: This AI-powered chatbot is like a pocket-sized therapist, offering cognitive behavioral therapy (CBT) through engaging conversations. It helps users identify negative thought patterns, develop coping strategies, and track their mood with unwavering support.

Ginger: This digital platform blends AI-powered self-guided care with virtual therapy sessions led by licensed professionals. It's like having a personal mental health coach who tailors exercises and content to your specific needs, while also providing access to human expertise when needed.

Mind strong: Imagine a world where your smartphone becomes a silent guardian of your mental health. Mind strong uses subtle cues like typing speed and sleep patterns to detect early signs of distress, alerting clinicians to potential issues before they escalate.

The Symphony of Hope: Benefits of the Human-AI Partnership

This harmonious collaboration between humans and AI holds the promise of a brighter future for mental healthcare:

Increased Accessibility: Breaking down barriers of distance and cost, making mental healthcare available to everyone, everywhere.

Early Detection and Prevention: Identifying subtle warning signs and intervening before a crisis erupts.

Personalized Treatment: Tailoring treatment plans to individual needs, like a bespoke suit for the mind.

Reduced Stigma: Offering anonymous and confidential support, encouraging people to seek help without fear of judgment.

Improved Efficiency: Streamlining workflows, freeing up clinicians to focus on what they do best: connecting with their patients on a human level.

The Human Touch: A Constant in the Equation

While AI is transforming mental healthcare, it's important to remember that the human touch remains irreplaceable. The therapeutic alliance between clinician and patient, built on empathy, trust, and understanding, is still the cornerstone of effective care.

AI is not here to replace human connection, but to enhance it. It's a tool that empowers clinicians to provide even more compassionate and effective care, ultimately helping us to better understand and heal the human mind.

About Author

I am bestselling author. Data scientist. I have proven technical skills (MBA, ACCA (Knowledge Level), BBA, several Google certifications) to deliver insightful books with ten years of business experience. I have written and published 400 books as per Goodreads record.

ORCID: https://orcid.org/0009-0004-8629-830X

Azhar.sario@hotmail.co.uk

www.ingramcontent.com/pod-product-compliance
Lightning Source LLC
Chambersburg PA
CBHW031419210526
45464CB00005B/1964